1000 BIBLE FACTS

Publications International, Ltd.

Let's get social!

 @Publications_International

 @PublicationsInternational

www.pilbooks.com

1.

Genesis 1 and 2 tell us that God created animals before humans, that he gave humans responsibility to be good stewards over the animals, and that Adam gave names to them.

2.

Along with the tree of knowledge of good and evil, the tree of life also grew in the garden of Eden. Genesis 2:9 says, "And out of the ground made the Lord God to grow every tree that is pleasant to the sight, and good for food; the tree of life also in the midst of the garden, and the tree of knowledge of good and evil."

3.

God placed the tree of life in the garden of Eden as a symbol of eternal life. After Adam and Eve sinned, God now longer allowed them access to it.

4.

Havilah was the first land, outside of Eden, mentioned in the Bible. Genesis 2:11 notes that this land was encompassed by Pison, one of the rivers that went out of Eden.

5.

The four rivers associated with the garden of Eden are the Euphrates, Hiddekel, Gihon, and Pison (Genesis 2:11–14).

6.

Ethiopia is encompassed by the river Gihon. Genesis 2:13 reads, "And the name of the second river is Gihon: the same is it that compasseth the whole land of Ethiopia."

7.

You probably noticed at an early age that the word *woman* contains the word *man*. According to Genesis 2:23, this is no accident. "She shall be called Woman," Adam said, "Because she was taken out of Man."

8.

A "helpmate" usually refers to a wife, in her role as helper to her husband. The word has arisen from the rendering of two Hebrew words in Genesis 2:18, where God says, "I will make [Adam] an help meet for him." However, "meet" in seventeenth-century English meant "appropriate" or "fit for."

9.

Adam's name is related to the word for ground (Hebrew *adamah*). Undoubtedly, this involves a play on words, since Adam was formed from "dust of the ground" (Genesis 2:7).

10.

Eve's name in Hebrew means "life" (*chavvah*). Adam called his wife Eve "because she was the mother of all living" (Genesis 3:20).

11.

The words "Ashes to ashes, dust to dust" are adapted from God's words to Adam in Genesis 3:19, reminding him that he was formed out of the ground and would return there: "for dust thou art, and unto dust shalt thou return."

12.

Snakes are mentioned in the Bible mostly as symbols, usually as threats. Evil entered the world through Satan in the form of a snake (Genesis 3), and wicked people are often compared to snakes or their venom. The threat of great harm is often compared to a snakebite.

13.

After Eve ate the forbidden fruit in the Garden of Eden, God told the serpent Satan that there would be "enmity" between serpents and women, and that her offspring "shall bruise thy head" (Genesis 3:15). This is the first promise of Jesus in the Bible.

14.

Before Adam and Eve sinned, they did not wear clothes and they were not embarrassed. But after they sinned, they were ashamed and made clothes for themselves out of fig leaves, which were not very substantial (Genesis 3:7).

15.

After God told Adam and Eve of the consequences of eating from the fruit of the tree of the knowledge of good and evil, he made them "coats of skins, and clothed them." These clothes, made out of animal skins, symbolized the animal sacrifices that would have to be offered for sin (Genesis 3:21).

16.

Adam had an unknown number of children. Cain, Abel, and Seth are the only named children, but Genesis 5:4 says, "And the days of Adam after he had begotten Seth were eight hundred years: and he begat sons and daughters."

17.

"Am I my brother's keeper?" was the response of Cain—who killed his brother Abel—when God came to him and asked him where Abel was (Genesis 4:9). He was attempting to deflect or escape responsibility for his crime. People wanting to avoid responsibility often use the phrase today.

18.

In many ancient societies, the relative of someone who was killed had the right to take vengeance for the death. Cain feared for his life because of this when he killed Abel. The law of Moses accommodated this practice, but carefully regulated it. The law distinguishes between accidental and deliberate homicide, provides cities of refuge, and requires approval of council elders before vengeance can be taken.

19.

Seth was the third son of Adam and Eve. Eve said God "appointed me another seed instead of Abel, whom Cain slew" (Genesis 4:25).

20.

The first 11 chapters of Genesis sweep through millennia of human experience, and include many names you won't read elsewhere. The life spans seem incredibly long, but interestingly, these long life spans all came before the great flood. Afterward, very few people lived more than 120 years.

21.

The Bible's oldest man was Methuselah. Methuselah lived to be 969 years old (Genesis 5:27).

22.

Jared, the second oldest man in the Bible, lived to the age of 962 (Genesis 5:20).

23.

Methuselah and Jared were not unique for their time. Noah lived for 950 years, Seth lived for 912 years, Enosh lived for 905 years, and Mahalalel lived for 895 years. The first man, Adam, lived for 930 years.

24.

Only two characters in the Bible never died: Enoch and Elijah. "Enoch walked with God: and he was not; for God took him" (Genesis 5:24). Elijah the prophet was taken to heaven in a fiery chariot without dying (2 Kings 2).

25.

Enoch was 365 years old when "God took him" (Genesis 5:21–24).

26.

God told Noah to build the ark 300 cubits long and 50 cubits wide. A cubit was a common measurement in ancient times, based on the distance from a grown man's elbow to the tip of his middle finger. The standard cubit was approximately 17.5 inches long, which would make Noah's ark about 440 feet by 73 feet—about the size of your average football field.

27.

All the animals did not enter Noah's ark two by two; some boarded the boat in parties of 14.

28.

The Bible mentions dozens of animals, wild and domestic, in many different contexts. Almost 180 Hebrew terms exist for animals, and more than 50 Greek terms. Unfortunately, not all the terms can be identified with certainty, and many animals have become extinct since biblical times.

29.

The Bible mentions some 50 types of birds. More than 350 species of birds are identified today in Palestine. Birds are included among sacrificial animals and among clean (edible) and unclean animals. They can be found in numerous stories in the Bible, including the story of the doves and the raven of Noah's ark.

30.

How did the olive branch acquire its reputation as a symbol of peace? The imagery might come from the story of Noah in Genesis 8:1–12. After the rain stopped, the floodwaters were still high. Noah sent out a dove to assess the situation, and it brought back an olive leaf, indicating that some trees were above water. So the olive branch became connected with the dove in a message of peace and renewal.

31.

The dove is best remembered as the bird that informed Noah that the waters of the Flood were receding. However, the dove wasn't the first animal released from the ark—that honor goes to the raven, which angered Noah by flying back and forth rather than doing the job it was assigned.

32.

The raven is the largest member of the crow family. It was one of the unclean animals (Leviticus 11:15). God's care for the raven was a symbol of his care for his people, and it also was a symbol of judgment and desolation.

33.

Noah's ark finally came to rest "in the seventh month, on the seventeenth day of the month, upon the mountains of Ararat" (Genesis 8:4). Per Genesis 8:5, the tops of the mountains were seen in the tenth month.

34.

Originally, humans were vegetarians, but after Noah's Flood, God gave animals for food as well. Animals were also used for transportation, in working the fields, as sacrificial animals, in the military, and as pets.

35.

Genesis 10:10 mentions the land of Shinar. This might be another name for Sumer, a nation that dominated the Tigris and Euphrates region in the third millennium B.C. The Sumerians were the world's first literate people. They invented cuneiform—triangular symbols pressed into wet clay with a reed stylus.

36.

Genesis 10:8–9 says that Nimrod was "a mighty one in the earth. He was a mighty hunter before the Lord." He had a great kingdom that included several cities in Babylonia and Assyria. The Bible says that he built Nineveh as well.

37.

Assyria is mentioned many times in the Bible. Assyria is located in Mesopotamia. Though its borders fluctuated greatly over time, its core territory was along the Tigris River.

38.

The Chaldeans appear frequently in the Old Testament. Chaldea was a region of southeastern Mesopotamia that bordered the head of the Persian Gulf, overlapping modern-day Iraq.

39.

Abram was originally from Ur. The ancient city of Ur was located near the mouth of the Euphrates, on its western bank (Genesis 11:31).

40.

Although Ur was a coastal city when it was built, the Euphrates river has since changed course. Ur's ruins are in a desert.

41.

For the most part, deserts in Bible lands do not have the great shifting sand dunes that are found in many deserts. Most of these deserts are dry, flat, and rocky. The hot desert winds blow fine dust or sand across the barren surface. Occasionally oases with springs and palm trees can be found.

42.

Genesis 11:31 tells of Abram leaving Ur of the Chaldees. He traveled with his nephew Lot, his wife Sarai, and his father Terah.

43.

As Lot and his family fled the destruction of Sodom and Gomorrah, Lot's wife looked back and was turned to a pillar of salt. The towering salt cliffs of Jebel Usdum (Mount Sodom) and the salt pillars at the southern end of the sea have been associated in tradition with this event. One distinctive 60-foot-high pillar is even called Lot's Wife.

44.

While there are many caves in Palestine, the Old Testament does not mention anyone living in them except in emergencies. Lot and his two daughters lived in a cave after Sodom and Gomorrah were destroyed. David and Elijah both hid in caves when their lives were in danger. And the prophet Obadiah hid 100 prophets of the Lord from the wicked queen Jezebel in two caves.

45.

The first battle mentioned in the Bible took place at the vale of Siddim (Genesis 14:3, 8, 10).

46.

Genesis 14 mentions that the battle that took place in the vale of Siddim was between multiple kings. The kings were rebelling against Chedorlaomer, a king of Elam.

47.

The vale of Siddim, near the Dead Sea, had slimepits in its landscape. Genesis 14:10 states that "the kings of Sodom and Gomorrah fled, and fell there."

48.

Melchizedek was not only a king of Salem, but also a "priest of the most high God" (Genesis 14:18).

49.

Abram rescued his brother's abducted son Lot near Hobah. Genesis 14:16 says, "And he brought back all the goods, and also brought again his brother Lot, and his goods, and the women also, and the people."

50.

Abram was 99 years old when the Lord appeared to him.

51.

Abraham's original name was Abram, which means "exalted father" or "the father is exalted." God gave him his new name, Abraham, which is explained as "father of many nations" (Genesis 17:3–5). This was to emphasize God's promise to Abraham that he would have many descendants.

52.

Abraham was the first person to be called a prophet in the Bible. In Genesis 20:1–14, God warned Abimelech, the king of Gerar, in a dream that the wife he had taken (Sarah) was actually married to a prophet (Abraham).

53.

The prophets of the Bible were men and women sent by God to speak for him to the people. Contrary to a popular stereotype, their major role was not to predict the future. Rather, they were sent to address contemporary situations. They often had very harsh words to say to kings and people, and, as a result, were usually not very popular.

54.

Ishmael was born to a maid of Abraham's wife. Because Abraham's wife, Sarah, could not bear a child, she offered her maid, Hagar, as a surrogate. Hagar gave birth to Ishmael (Genesis 16:15).

55.

When Sarah overheard the news that she would bear a son in her old age, she laughed (Genesis 18:12).

56.

Abraham was called to sacrifice his son in the mountainous region of Moriah. God relents in Genesis 22:12: "Lay not thine hand upon the lad, neither do thou any thing unto him: for now I know that thou fearest God, seeing thou hast not withheld thy son, thine only son from me."

57.

Abraham sent a servant to find a bride for his son Isaac, and it was that servant who gave Rebekah "a golden earring of half a shekel weight, and two bracelets for her hands of ten shekels weight of gold" (Genesis 24:22).

58.

Isaac's wife, Rebekah, was Syrian (Genesis 25:20).

59.

Unlike his father Abraham, Isaac did not travel to Egypt during a time of famine. Rather, Genesis 26:1–6 notes that the Lord urged Isaac to live among the Philistines in Gerar.

60.

Genesis 20 and 26 tell similar stories about Abraham and Isaac trying to pass off their wives as their sisters in Gerar, a Philistine city. This was for fear of the Philistine king, Abimelech, who they thought would kill them in order to take their wives. The events were separated by many years, however, and the two Abimelechs may have been different people.

61.

The Cave of Machpelah was the cave that Abraham bought to bury his wife Sarah in, near Hebron (Genesis 23). Abraham, Isaac, and Jacob also were buried there. Abraham's purchase was significant, since it represented the first clear title to the land that God had promised him.

62.

After Sarah's death, Abraham took Keturah as a wife. She gave birth to six sons, including Midian, ancestor of the Midianites (Genesis 25:1–2).

63.

When the once-barren Rebekah finally conceived, the children "struggled together within her." The Lord told Rebekah that there were two nations in her womb, "and the one people shall be stronger than the other people; and the elder shall serve the younger (Genesis 25:21–26).

64.

Esau and Jacob were twins. Jacob followed Esau out of the womb and took hold of his twin's heel (Genesis 25:24–26).

65.

Jacob and his twin brother, Esau, did not get along well for much of their lives, because Jacob took Esau's birthright. Their descendants were the Israelites and the Edomites, respectively, groups that continued to feud throughout their histories. (Genesis 25:22).

66.

When Rebekah wanted to fool Isaac into believing Jacob was Esau, a "hairy man," she "put the skins of the kids of the goats upon his hands, and upon the smooth of his neck" (Genesis 27:16).

67.

Jacob was traveling from Beersheba toward Haran when he stopped for the night and dreamed of the ladder of heaven. "And he called the name of that place Bethel: but the name of that city was called Luz at the first" (Genesis 28:19).

68.

The Hebrews used large standing stone slabs to commemorate important events or covenants. Jacob used a stone for a pillow at Bethel, and then set it up as a memorial of his encounter with God and poured oil on it. The Canaanites erected standing stones for worship, but the Israelites were prohibited from using these. An impressive set of 10 pillars still stands at a sacred Canaanite site at biblical Gezer.

69.

When Rebekah's nurse, Deborah, died, she was buried under an oak tree in Bethel (Genesis 35:8).

70.

Jacob loved Rachel, and agreed to serve her father, Laban, for seven years to gain her hand in marriage. After the seven years, Laban deceived Jacob into marrying Rachel's older sister, Leah, instead. After a week, Jacob was allowed to take Rachel as a wife, although he agreed to another seven years working for Laban (Genesis 29:16–32).

71.

Leah's son Reuben found mandrakes in the field and brought them to her (Genesis 30:14). The mandrake plant appears in Genesis 30 and then again in the Song of Solomon 7:13.

72.

When Jacob and his wives fled the household of Laban, who felt that Jacob's success had come at his expense, Jacob's wife Rachel took her father Laban's household gods from his home (Genesis 31).

73.

When Rachel took with her the family's household gods and hid them under her saddle, her father, Laban, was alarmed enough to come after her and retrieve them (Genesis 31). These were small idols kept in private households to consult about the future.

74.

After God hearkened to Rachel, Jacob's beloved wife, and "opened her womb," she bore a son named Joseph (Genesis 30:22–25).

75.

Rachel died giving birth to Benjamin. As he was born, she named him *Benoni* which means "son of my sorrow," but he was renamed Benjamin ("son of the right hand") by his father (Genesis 35).

76.

After raping Dinah, Shechem told his father to "Get me this damsel to wife." Hamor suggested to Jacob that their tribes intermarry. Jacob's sons, furious that their sister had been defiled, demanded all males in Hamor's tribe be circumcised before they could marry Israelite women. Three days after the circumcisions, Dinah's brothers killed Shechem, Hamor, and all the men of their city (Genesis 34:1–26).

77.

The sons of Bilhah, Rachel's handmaid, were Dan and Naphtali. Gad and Asher were the sons of Zilpah, Leah's handmaid (Genesis 35:25–26).

78.

Tamar disguised herself, pretended to be a harlot, and lured her father-in-law, Judah. Tamar demanded Judah's signet as a pledge of payment. A pregnant Tamar was brought before Judah for punishment. When Judah saw his signet and realized he was the father of Tamar's twin sons, he repented (Genesis 38:6–26).

79.

The midwife was the Israelite equivalent of a visiting nurse or public health worker. The Hebrews had professional midwives when they lived in Egypt who refused to obey the pharaoh's orders to kill Hebrew baby boys (Exodus 1). A midwife also helped Tamar when she had trouble giving birth to twins (Genesis 38).

80.

In biblical times, the primary occupations were the ones that provided the basics: food and shelter. Farmers provided food, shepherds and ranchers provided meat, skins, and wool, and fishermen made profits in coastal areas. In general, women prepared and cooked the food, and made cloth out of animal hair, which they used to make clothes and tents.

81.

Tamar had twin sons, the elder of which, Pharez, was an ancestor of Jesus (Genesis 38:24–30).

82.

Jacob wrestled one night with a stranger whom he recognized as God's representative, and he asked him for a blessing. The man then bestowed a new name upon him.

83.

God gave Jacob a new name, Israel. This name means "he strives with God" or "God strives" (Genesis 35:10).

84.

Jacob favored Joseph over all his children, as he was the "son of his old age" (Genesis 37:1–3).

85.

While Joseph's other brothers wanted to kill him, Reuben suggested they throw Joseph in a cistern. He intended to rescue Joseph and restore him to their father Jacob later. When a caravan passes, however, Judah suggests selling Joseph to the merchants instead (Genesis 37:21–27).

86.

The Midianites sold Joseph to Potiphar, an officer of Pharaoh and captain of the guard (Genesis 37:36).

87.

In Genesis 40, Joseph tells Pharaoh's butler in prison that Pharaoh will "lift up thine head, and restore thee unto thy place." He tells Pharaoh's baker that Pharaoh will "lift up thy head off thee, and shall hang thee on a tree." His predictions of rescue for one man and death for the other were accurate.

88.

On being restored to favor, the butler did not immediately tell Pharaoh of the man who had interpreted his dream because "Yet did not the chief butler remember Joseph, but forgat him" (Genesis 40:23). It was two years later that the pharaoh had a dream that required interpretation, and the butler remembered Joseph and brought him to Pharaoh's attention.

89.

In the story of Joseph, Pharaoh dreamt of seven fat kine (cattle) being eaten by seven skinny, starving cows. This indicated that famine would follow a time of plenty (Genesis 41:1–4).

90.

Life in biblical times was tightly bound up with the cycle of the seasons and the availability of food. People lived with the worry that they were one bad year away from starvation. Joseph made a name for himself when he warned the pharaoh about an impending seven-year famine. He organized food storage and distribution programs to combat it (Genesis 41).

91.

Pharaoh gave the name "Zaphnathpaaneah" to Joseph (Genesis 41:45).

92.

Bread was an important food staple in biblical times, and there are hundreds of references to bread in the Bible, over 20 in the book of Genesis alone. The word bread is often used to mean "food" in the Bible, as in Genesis 41:54, in the story of Joseph: "the dearth was in all lands, but in the land of Egypt there was bread."

93.

When Joseph's brothers came seeking food in Egypt, Joseph demanded that Simeon stay in prison in Egypt while the other brothers went and brought Benjamin to Egypt.

94.

Joseph's father, Jacob, gave Joseph's brothers a present of rare delicacies that included almonds to take to their brother (Genesis 43:11). The blooming of almond trees in late January is a sign that spring is coming. Almonds served as models for the cups of the golden lampstand at the tabernacle.

95.

Oil lamps were the common means of lighting in biblical homes. They were made of clay or iron, and they burned olive oil for fuel. Thousands of oil lamps have been found from all periods. Early lamps were flat bowls, and then a spout began to evolve with a pinched edge at the rim. Later lamps had a hole for the wick.

96.

Joseph told Pharaoh in Genesis 47:1 that his family had come to the land of Goshen. Goshen is located in modern-day Egypt.

97.

Jacob, from his deathbed, compared his son Judah to a lion (Genesis 49:9).

98.

Were there doctors in the Old Testament? Absolutely. We think of medicine as modern science, but there have always been those who specialized in healing arts. For instance, Joseph enlisted doctors to embalm his father, Jacob (Genesis 50:2). And in Israel, King Asa of Judah sought medical help when he had a foot ailment (2 Chronicles 16:12).

99.

Embalming was not done in Israel; it was a distinctively Egyptian invention, and it was usually reserved for kings and persons of some repute. Two individuals are mentioned in the Bible as having been embalmed: Joseph, a Hebrew who had risen high in the Egyptian court, and his father, Jacob.

100.

The twelve tribes of Israel were named after the sons or grandsons of Jacob: Benjamin, Ephraim, Manasseh, Naphtali, Dan, Asher, Issachar, Judah, Zebulon, Simeon, Reuben, and Gad. While no tribe was named after Jacon's son Joseph, two tribes were named after Joseph's sons Manasseh and Ephraim (Genesis 48).

101.

The word *exodus* means "a way out." So, as you would guess, the book by that name is an escape story. Specifically, this book tells how the Israelites left Egypt. Exodus also includes the Ten Commandments, given at Mount Sinai.

102.

After hiding Moses for three months, Jochebed put him in an "ark of bulrushes" by the river. When the pharaoh's daughter found the basket, Miriam, Moses' sister, stepped forward and offered to find a Hebrew nurse for the child. Jochebed was paid to nurse her own son until he was weaned (Exodus 2:2–10).

103.

Following his killing of an Egyptian, Moses fled from the wrath of Pharaoh to Midian, a region located in the northwestern Arabian Desert (Exodus 2:15).

104.

Ramses II was one of Egypt's greatest pharaohs, reigning for 67 years in the thirteenth century B.C. Many scholars believe he was the pharaoh who gave Moses such a hard time regarding the Israelites' exodus from Egypt. Ramses II built many great temples, including the astounding temple complex in the sandstone cliffs at Abu Simbel on the Nile River.

105.

Moses—who was called upon more than once to talk of weighty matters—was likely a stutterer. In the Bible, he claims to be "slow of speech," which suggests some kind of speech impediment.

106.

When Moses asked God what his name was, God responded with this cryptic phrase: "I am that I am" (Exodus 3:14). God may have been revealing something profound about himself, or he also may have been reminding Moses of his earlier promise that "Certainly I will be with thee" (verse 12).

107.

The plague of blood, in which the water sources of Egypt turned to blood, was the first plague (Exodus 7:14–24).

108.

The Egyptian magicians in Moses' day were able to duplicate the first two plagues that God sent upon Egypt—turning the Nile to blood and producing frogs. They tried to duplicate the third plague—bringing forth gnats—but failed. They also were able to turn their rods into snakes, like Aaron did, but his "snake" devoured theirs.

109.

The Bible may be Holy Scripture, but it still contains contradictions. For example, in Genesis, it first says that man was created after the other animals (Genesis 1:25–27). Then it says man was created before the other animals (2:18–19). In Exodus, it first says that all of the (non-Hebrew) cattle and horses in Egypt died (Exodus 9:3–6), but later it is suggested that all of the pharaoh's horses did not die (14:9).

110.

The Bible mentions three instances of waters being miraculously parted. The Red Sea parted when Israel, led by Moses, was fleeing the Egyptians. The Jordan River parted twice, first when the Israelites under Joshua needed to cross it to enter the Promised Land, and then again when the prophets Elijah and Elisha needed to cross.

111.

Miriam was the first female prophet mentioned by name in the Bible (Exodus 15:20).

112.

Immediately after the Israelites crossed the Red Sea, Miriam and Moses led the people in song (Exodus 15).

113.

The prophetess Miriam said, "Sing ye to the Lord, for he hath triumphed gloriously; the horse and his rider hath he thrown into the sea" and led the women of Israel in a dance (Exodus 15:19–21).

114.

Prophetess is used five times in the Old Testament: Miriam (Exodus 15:20); Deborah (Judges 4:4); Huldah (2 Kings 22:14); Isaiah's wife, "the prophetess" (Isaiah 8:3); and Noadiah, a prophetess who opposed Nehemiah (Nehemiah 6:14). Deborah and Huldah exercised significant responsibilities.

115.

When Miriam led the women in song and dance, she used a timbrel, or tambourine (Exodus 15:20).

116.

After crossing the Red Sea, Moses led his people out into the wilderness. When they arrived at Marah, the water was too bitter to drink, so Moses threw a tree into the water in order to make it drinkable (Exodus 15:25).

117.

The Israelites were provided with "bread from heaven" in the wilderness. It appeared each morning as a fine, white, flaky substance on the ground that tasted like wafers and honey. Its name (Hebrew *man*) came from the puzzled Israelites, who asked "*man-hu?*" ("What is it?").

118.

Manna is described as tasting like wafer made with honey in Exodus 16:31. In Numbers 11:8, however, it's described as tasting like "fresh oil."

119.

During the Exodus, Israel defeated Amalek in Rephidim. This was the battle that Moses assisted in by holding up the rod of God (Exodus 17:8–13).

120.

The Mosaic law contains 613 specific commandments regulating most aspects of people's lives and worship, but this is not the earliest example of an ancient law code. The Sumerians developed the first such codes in the middle of the second millennium B.C. The most systematic law code was that of the Babylonian king Hammurabi (1792–1750 B.C.). The Hittites also developed an extensive law code in the thirteenth century B.C.

121.

Mosaic law established seven festivals. Three of these were great pilgrimage festivals that were related to the agricultural calendar: the feasts of Passover, Pentecost, and Tabernacles. The two high holy days (the Day of Atonement and New Year's Day) and two days of rest (the Sabbath and the New Moon festival) completed the festivals. The festivals of Purim and Hanukkah arose later.

122.

The Pentecost feast was so named because it comes 50 days after the first Sabbath of Passover—*pent* means 50. It is also known as the Feast of Weeks, First Fruits, or Harvest. It was a spring festival celebrating the completion of the grain harvest.

123.

The Sabbath day was very important. Not only could people rest and be refreshed, but also they were reminded of God's Creation (Exodus 20:11). If people defiantly disobeyed God and worked on this day, the penalty was death (Exodus 31:15, 35:2). In fact, Numbers 15:32–36 tell of a man found gathering wood on the Sabbath who was stoned to death.

124.

The penalities stated in Exodus 21:23–25 concerning an eye for an eye or a life for a life sound barbaric to many people today. However, the principle was very humane: Let the punishment fit the crime. In the ancient Near Eastern world, this limited the usual cycle of escalating retribution and revenge.

125.

The Law provided for the land to lie unplanted every seventh year (Exodus 23; Leviticus 25). This corresponded to the pattern of a weekly Sabbath for people, and it allowed the land needed time to rest. More importantly, whatever grew in the fields was to be left for the poor, and debts were canceled in the seventh year, allowing people a fresh start (Deuteronomy 15).

126.

As the Israelites wandered through the desert, they brought along a portable place of worship. God gave them detailed instructions for building a large tent—the tabernacle—that could be moved from place to place. The tabernacle was richly decorated with expensive fabrics, and there was a special place for the ark of the covenant and other sacred items.

127.

Israelite priests performed many, if not all, of their duties in the tabernacle and temple barefooted. This was because of the sacredness of the ground on which they walked. God also told Moses to remove his sandals at the burning bush: "Put off thy shoes from off thy feet, for the place whereon thou standest is holy ground" (Exodus 3:5).

128.

Priests' clothing was colorful and expensive (Exodus 28). Ordinary priests wore long linen tunics, turbans, and beautiful belts made of blue, purple, and scarlet cloth. The high priest wore an ornate breastplate made of gold and expensive linens. This had 12 precious stones on it—one for each tribe of Israel. The hem of his robe had small bells on it, which jingled as he walked.

129.

Jewelry is mentioned often in the Bible, and much has been found in excavations of Bible lands. Early in history, it was made of bone chips, shells, and colored stones. Later, precious stones and metals were used more often. Many gold and silver necklaces, bracelets, earrings, rings, and beautiful precious stones have been found.

130.

Israel's temple was carefully planned, including the details of its dimensions. It was an impressive structure, some 90 feet long, 45 feet wide, and 3 stories high. The innermost room, the Holy of Holies (or Most Holy Place), was where the ark of the covenant resided, symbolizing God's very presence. The ark's dimensions formed a perfect cube.

131.

Hebrew has two words that are translated as "ark" in English. The most common refers to the ark of the covenant. The rarer word refers to Noah's ark and is also used for the basket of bulrushes that the baby Moses was placed into, Moses' ark.

132.

The ark was Israel's most holy object. It was an ornate box made of acacia wood, overlaid with gold, and topped with a golden mercy seat flanked by two winged cherubs. It contained the tablets of the Ten Commandments, a pot of manna, and Aaron's rod. It was kept in the Most Holy Place of the tabernacle and temple, but the Babylonians destroyed it in 586 B.C.

133.

Moses received stone tablets containing the Ten Commandments on Mount Sinai (Exodus 31:18).

134.

The Bible claims to be the Word of God. Some passages, however, mention God's writing explicitly. The Ten Commandments were "written with the finger of God" (Exodus 31:18); they were "the writing of God" (Exodus 32:16). In 1 Chronicles 28:19, David said, "The Lord made me understand in writing by his hand upon me, even all the works of this pattern."

135.

In many passages, the Bible refers to books kept in heaven. Moses pleads with God to blot him out of the "book which thou hast written" (Exodus 32:32) for the sake of Israel's forgiveness. The book of Daniel speaks of the day when "the books were opened" (Daniel 7:10). And the book of Malachi speaks of a "book of remembrance" that was written about those who feared the Lord (Malachi 3:16).

136.

Tabernacle was another term for the tent. Its name indicates that it was a place where people could meet God. But there was also a separate tent called the "tabernacle of the congregation" (Exodus 33:7). This was a temporary tent that Moses used to pitch outside of the camp, where he and the people could also meet God. It was not known later in Israel's history.

137.

After communicating with God on Mount Sinai, Moses returned to camp with a shining face—a condition that frightened everyone who saw him. To keep everyone calm, Moses covered his face with a veil (Exodus 34:29–35).

138.

The book of Leviticus contains instructions for the Levites—the clergy for whom the book is named—and others concerning holiness. Many laws relate to animal sacrifice, but every law is related in some way to the need for personal holiness and blamelessness in relationship with God and with others. It contains the famous passage about loving one's neighbor as oneself (Leviticus 19:18).

139.

Many people add salt to their meals as seasoning. Would it surprise you to know that the sacrifices of the Israelites were also seasoned with salt? "Neither shalt thou suffer the salt of the covenant of thy God to be lacking from thy meat offering" (Leviticus 2:13). Since salt was a preservative, it symbolized eternity.

140.

Doves and pigeons were the most important birds in the Old Testament. They were used often in sacrifices. When pigeons were used, they were always "young pigeons" (Leviticus 1:14). Noah sent out three doves from the ark to find land; the second brought back an olive leaf, a symbol of new life.

141.

No fewer than eight species of owls have been tentatively identified from the lists of unclean birds in Leviticus and Deuteronomy, including the eagle owl, short- and long-eared owls, wood owl, fisher owl, screech owl, little owl, and scops owl. The eagle owl is the world's largest, measuring up to 28 inches long.

142.

Leviticus 11:29–30 mentions several animals that are unclean, some of them reptiles. They include the tortoise, the chameleon, and the lizard. These all were among the "creeping things that creep upon the earth." Lizards were (and are) common in Palestine.

143.

Hebrew had only one word for domesticated pigs and wild boars. Both were on the lists of prohibited foods in Leviticus 11 and Deuteronomy 14. Psalm 80:13 refers clearly to the wild boar: "The boar out of the woods doth waste [Israel]."

144.

Did you know that the word *scapegoat* comes from the Bible? Leviticus 16 describes a ritual involving two goats. One was sacrificed as a sin offering. The other was released into the desert after Israel's sins were symbolically transferred onto its head. The Bible calls this animal the "scapegoat" (Leviticus 16:8). Eventually, the word came to refer to anyone who takes the blame for others.

145.

The law of Moses had many humane provisions for the poor, widows, orphans, and the like. One stated that farmers should not harvest every corner of their fields or vineyards, nor should they pick up what had fallen during the reaping process. These were to be left for the poor (Leviticus 19:9–10). We see Boaz putting this into practice in a heartwarming story in Ruth 2.

146.

The book of Numbers is about preparations for Israel to enter the land of Canaan. The people are numbered, more instructions are given, and the starts and stops of their journey to the Promised Land are detailed, including the 38 years of wandering in the wilderness.

147.

The book of Numbers begins with the Lord commanding Moses to take a census.

148.

The Lord decreed that people who took a vow as a Nazirite were prohibited from eating anything that came from the grapevine: "All the days of his separation shall he eat nothing that is made of the vine tree, from the kernels even to the husk" (Numbers 6:4).

149.

While wandering the desert after their exodus from Egypt, the Israelites complained about how they missed "the fish. . . the cucumbers, and the melons, and the leeks, and the onions, and the garlick" (Numbers 11:5).

150.

Quail are mentioned in connection with only one event in the Bible. When the Israelites were in the wilderness, God sent quail into the camp in the evening and the people collected them for food. Quail are small game birds that migrate, but they can only do so with the help of the wind. The Bible states that they did come in on the wind (Numbers 11:31).

151.

Both Miriam and Aaron, claiming that they were equals of Moses as prophets, spoke out against their brother. But only Miriam became leprous. Another reason they spoke out against Moses was that he had married an Ethiopian woman (Numbers 12:1–10).

152.

Moses' father-in-law, Jethro, had other names. In Exodus, he is initially referred to as Reuel (2:16–18), priest of Midian and father of seven daughters, but then as Jethro (3:1). In Numbers 10:29, the same man is called "Hobab, the son of Raguel the Midianite."

153.

Moses was commanded to send out one man from each of the twelve tribes of Israel to explore the land of Canaan (Numbers 13:1–16).

154.

Moses' brother Aaron, the high priest, had a very interesting rod. On one occasion, it turned into a snake that devoured the Egyptian magicians' rods/snakes (Exodus 7:12). On another, it sprouted buds, blossoms, and almonds overnight; this was in a contest with the rebellious people concerning priestly authority (Numbers 17:8).

155.

Folk songs around the world arise from everyday life, and even the Bible records some. One was sung to commemorate a well: "Spring up, O well; sing ye unto it: The princes digged the well, the nobles of the people digged it, by the direction of the lawgiver, with their staves." (Numbers 21:17–18).

156.

Balaam holds the dubious distinction of being the only biblical character to have had a conversation with a donkey. Balaam was a prophet and magician who was hired by Balak, an enemy of Israel, to curse Israel. On his way there, his donkey balked at going on because it saw an angel and was fearful. The donkey even spoke to Balaam about this, according to Numbers 22:28–30.

157.

When the Israelites took over Jerusalem, its many gods and pagan culture offended them, and so they gave its name a new meaning, "City of Peace." This title has remained a symbol of people's hopes for the city ever since.

158.

After Israel inherited the land of Canaan, one of its top priorities was to drive out the Canaanites. God repeatedly warned them of the dangers of mixing with them. At one point, he stated that they would be "pricks in your eyes, and thorns in your sides" (Numbers 33:55).

159.

Israel is bordered to the west by the Mediterranean Sea. In the Bible, it is usually referred to as "the great sea." For example, Numbers 34:6 says, "And as for the western border, ye shall even have the great sea for a border: this shall be your west border."

160.

The title of the book of Deuteronomy means "second law." The book repeats and adds to many of the laws found in Exodus, Leviticus, and Numbers. The laws are framed by Moses' last addresses to the people of Israel, in which he reviews God's gracious dealings with them in the wilderness. Moses urges them to live faithful lives in their new land, Canaan.

161.

Although not part of the Promised Land, Heshbon was taken by the Israelites when its ruler, Sihon, would not permit them to pass (Deuteronomy 2:24–34).

162.

Og, king of Bashan (an area northeast of the Jordan River), opposed the Israelites when they wanted to pass through his land (Deuteronomy 3). He was a giant of a man. His bed was made of iron, and it was on display in Rabbah, capital of the Ammonites, for many years. It was more than 13 feet long and 6 feet wide!

163.

Fish were an abundant source of food in all Bible lands. The law of Moses (Deuteronomy 14:9–10) allowed eating whatever has "fins and scales" (most fish), but it prohibited eating whatever did not have these (thus excluding sharks, eels, rays, water mammals, reptiles, and invertebrates).

164.

Priests were the primary religious authorities in Israel, but the kings also had religious duties. They were supposed to be examples for the people. They were to read and obey the Law and lead people in doing the same (Deuteronomy 17).

165.

Deuteronomy 17:14–20 lists the qualifications and duties of a king: God must choose him, he must be an Israelite, he must not multiply horses for himself (i.e., rely on his army, with its horses and chariots), he must not multiply wives (who might turn his heart away from God), he must not accumulate too much wealth, and he must know and keep the Law.

166.

The Law provided for certain people to escape military service under certain circumstances (Deuteronomy 20). These included those who had built a house and not yet dedicated it, and those who had planted a vineyard and not yet enjoyed its fruits.

167.

Military exemptions applied to anyone who was engaged to be married (Deuteronomy 20:7). Futhermore, newlywed men were to be exempted from military service or any other business for a full year. This allowed for a good start to the marriage (24:5).

168.

It was common in ancient times (as well as in modern times) to yoke an ox and a donkey together to pull a plow. However, Mosaic law prohibited this (Deuteronomy 22:10). While this may have been primarily for its moral lesson, it also was humane, since the two animals are not well matched for joint work.

169.

In biblical times, if someone made a loan and a cloak or something else was put up as collateral, the lender was to respect the borrower's dignity by not entering his house to seize the collateral. He had to wait outside for the borrower to bring it out. If the borrower was poor, the lender also had to return the cloak each night, since that was what the borrower slept in (Deuteronomy 24:10–13).

170.

In Deuteronomy 31, the Lord instructed Moses to write a song and teach it to the children of Israel shortly before his death: "For the Lord's portion is his people; Jacob is the lot of his inheritance. He found him in a desert land, and in the waste howling wilderness; he led him about, he instructed him, he kept him as the apple of his eye" (Deuteronomy 32:9–10).

171.

Moses was allowed to see the Promised Land from Mount Nebo (Deuteronomy 32:49).

172.

Moses was buried in a valley in the land of Moab (Deuteronomy 34:6).

173.

The book of Joshua focuses entirely on the land of Canaan and the Israelites' possession of it as the fulfillment of God's promise to Abraham. Moses' successor, Joshua, led Israel into the land, did battle with the Canaanites at Jericho and elsewhere, and portioned the land to the 12 tribes of Israel.

174.

The harlot Rahab offered lodging to the spies sent by Joshua and hid them. But when asked by the king of Jericho, Rahab claimed not to know where they were (Joshua 2:1–5).

175.

The Israelites who spied on the land of Jericho and were hidden by Rahab told her to put a red cord in her window so that her household would be spared in the battle that followed (Joshua 2:17–18).

176.

Joshua brought the Israelites into the Promised Land across the Jordan River—specifically, the Jordan's riverbed (Joshua 3:17).

177.

When the priests carrying the ark of the covenant led the way across the Jordan River, the river stopped flowing. Joshua 3:17 notes that the "Israelites passed over on dry ground."

178.

The first place the Israelites encamped in the land of Canaan after they had crossed the Jordan River was Gilgal. They named the site "Gilgal" in a wordplay on the reproach of Egypt that was finally rolled away (Joshua 5:9). The Hebrew word for "to roll" is *galal.*

179.

A spring waters Jericho, which was first occupied in 9000 B.C. It was an oasis in the Jordan Valley, and was called the City of Palms in the Bible. The Israelites captured it under Joshua, in the famous incident when its walls collapsed.

180.

Six days of trumpet-blowing perambulations took place before Jericho's defensive wall came down. When Joshua sent the priests to blow their trumpets on the seventh day, the people joined in with their own shouting—and Jericho's wall collapsed (Joshua 6).

181.

Joshua's curse on Jericho stated that anyone rebuilding Jericho would pay a stiff price: "He shall lay the foundation thereof in his firstborn, and in his youngest son shall he set up the gates of it" (Joshua 6:26). Many years later, a man named Hiel, from Bethel, did some rebuilding, and it cost him his oldest and youngest sons, in fulfillment of this prophecy (1 Kings 16:34).

182.

Achan was the man who caused the Israelites their only defeat when they entered the land of Canaan (Joshua 7). When they took Jericho, they were to set aside everything to God for destruction. However, Achan's greed got the best of him, and he hid some goods in his tent. As a result, Israel was defeated in their next battle, at the tiny outpost of Ai.

183.

Thanks to an ambush suggested by God, Joshua was able to destroy the city of Ai. Joshua 8 states that 30,000 of Joshua's men hid behind a hill while the rest of the Israelites drew out the people of Ai. Once the city was deserted, Joshua's men set it on fire.

184.

God often used insects as weapons. For example, it is said that he sent swarms of hornets into the land of Canaan ahead of the Israelites to drive out their enemies. Whether this is a literal or symbolic reference remains open to debate.

185.

After describing one of Joshua's exploits, the text says, "Is not this written in the Book of Jasher?" (Joshua 10:13). Apart from two references to this book, we have no information about this historian.

186.

Joshua captured a total of thirty-one kings (Joshua 12:9–24).

187.

Fathers were responsible for their whole households, including servants, in religious matters. Fathers were the ones who would bring the sacrifices to the priests. Joshua spoke for everyone in his household when he said that he and his house would serve the Lord (Joshua 24:15).

188.

Almost all Israelite houses during Old Testament times were made of mud bricks. The walls were coated with waterproof plaster on the inside. The floors were made of hard-packed clay, and wealthier homes had floors paved with smooth stones. Roofs were made from wooden beams covered in branches, which were filled in with mud plaster to make a flat surface.

189.

Joshua was buried "in the border of his inheritance in Timnathheres, in the mount of Ephraim, on the north side of the hill Gaash" (Judges 2:9).

190.

The book of Judges tells a story of a repeated cycle of the nation's sin, enslavement, and deliverance by warrior-judges. The cycle spirals downward, however, and by the end of the book things are so bad that the author despairingly says, "in those days there was no king in Israel: every man did that which was right in his own eyes" (Judges 21:25).

191.

Eglon, the king of Moab, was so fat that when Ehud thrust a blade into his belly, the fat closed upon the blade and Ehud couldn't remove it (Judges 3:17–22).

192.

The Kishon river was the site of a battle between Israel (led by Barak) and the Canaanites (led by Sisera). The prophet Deborah initiated this battle, telling Barak, "And I will draw unto thee to the river Kishon Sisera, the captain of Jabin's army, with his chariots and his multitude; and I will deliver him into thine hand" (Judges 4:7).

193.

The prophetess Deborah was the wife of Lapidoth (Judges 4:4).

194.

Jael killed Sisera, the Canaanite general, by driving a tent nail into his temples (Judges 4:21–22).

195.

After the downfall of Sisera, Deborah and Barak sang and praised God for avenging Israel (Judges 5:1–3).

196.

Hebrew poetry can be very dramatic. The poetic description of the death of Sisera shows an awful death struggle: "At her feet he bowed, he fell, he lay down; At her feet he bowed, he fell; where he bowed, there he fell down dead" (Judges 5:27).

197.

Deborah was a prophetess, a female judge, and described herself as "a mother in Israel" (Judges 5:7).

198.

Deborah's title, "a mother in Israel," refers to her leadership over Israel (Judges 5:7). Israel had been quietly submitting to its enemies in those days, and it was not until Deborah arose as "a mother in Israel" that Israel began to have hope again. She provided the impetus and leadership for action and eventual victory.

199.

When Gideon was called by the Lord to rescue Israel, he asked for several signs from the Lord, and they were given to him. These included his sacrifice of meat and bread being consumed by fire, a wool fleece left overnight gathering dew even though the ground was dry, and a wool fleece left overnight remaining dry even though the ground was wet with dew (Judges 6:11–40).

200.

Small armies fighting against overwhelming numbers are commonplace in the Bible, but Gideon wins the prize for most unlikely victory. He fought off 135,000 Midianite invaders with just 300 soldiers and 300 trumpets.

201.

Gideon was one of the heroes of the Bible: God gave him a great victory over the Midianites (Judges 7). He then properly refused an offer to make him king as a result. However, he was not perfect. He made an ephod—a garment worn by the high priest—and Israel committed idolatry by worshipping with it. Judges 8:27 states it "became a snare unto Gideon, and to his house."

202.

Before Samson's birth, an angel of the Lord appeared to his parents. The angel first appeared to Samson's mother, and then to both of his parents (Judges 13).

203.

Puzzling riddles were common in the biblical world. Only after the riddle was interpreted did its point become clear. A well-known riddle was Samson's: "Out of the eater came forth meat, and out of the strong came forth sweetness" (Judges 14:14). This referred to a lion he had killed and in whose carcass bees made honey. Because the riddle was answered, Samson killed 30 Philistines.

204.

Samson was responsible for the death of several thousand Philistines (Judges 14–16). This was helpful to the Israelites, since the Philistines were their major antagonists. Once, he even killed 1,000 men with the jawbone of a donkey. Shamgar was a lesser-known judge, but he too killed many Philistines: 600 of them with an ox goad (Judges 3:31).

205.

Before Samson told Delilah the truth behind the source of his strength, he told her three false tales: that he would become weak if tied up with seven green withs that had never been dried, that he could be tied up securely with new ropes that had never been used, and that he could be defeated if she wove his hair into a loom (Judges 16:1–22).

206.

Delilah was a Philistine from the valley of Sorek (Judges 16:3–5).

207.

The Old Testament records several actual incidents of cutting hair. Samson's lover Delilah betrayed him by having a man cut off his hair while Samson slept. Job shaved his head when he mourned. An Ammonite king humiliated David's servants by shaving half their beards. And Ezekiel was to shave his head and burn or scatter the hair in a symbolic act.

208.

Delilah has become famous as a symbol of a treacherous seductress, since she was Samson's lover and the one who betrayed him to the Philistines. She did this by coaxing from him the secret to his great strength, which was his long hair (Judges 16). Contrary to popular thought, she did not cut his hair, but rather held his sleeping head on her lap while a man she called in cut it.

209.

The book of Ruth is a literary masterpiece, a sparkling gem that tells a heartwarming story about a widowed woman (Naomi) and her daughter-in-law (Ruth), for whom things finally work out in the end. Ruth marries Boaz, who provides for them both. The family tree at the book's end connects Ruth with Abraham and shows her to be David's great-grandmother.

210.

The book of Ruth is the first book named after a woman in the Bible. The book of Esther appears later, after the book of Nehemiah. Ruth and Esther are the only books of the Bible named after women.

211.

Naomi, wife of Elimelech, only appears in the book of Ruth (Ruth 1–4).

212.

Naomi, Ruth's mother-in-law, lost her husband and her two sons. Her name means "pleasant," but she told people to call her *Mara*, which means "bitter" (Ruth 1:20). Fortunately, in the end, things were pleasant for Ruth and Naomi.

213.

The two sons of Noami and Elimelech were Mahlon and Chilion. The sons married two women of Moab, Ruth and Orpah (Ruth 1:2–4).

214.

When their husbands died, Naomi urged her daughters-in-law Orpah and Ruth to return to their mothers and search for new husbands. Orpah was eventually convinced to leave, but Ruth refused to abandon her mother-in-law Naomi (Ruth 1:8–18).

215.

When Boaz first met Ruth, he spoke to her of her kindness to Naomi, and offered her bread and vinegar at mealtime (Ruth 2).

216.

After the death of Ruth's husband, Mahlon, Boaz took her as a wife. Together they had a son, Obed, the father of Jesse and grandfather of David (Ruth 4:13, 17, 22).

217.

Boaz's kinsman gave up his claim to the land of Naomi's husband Elimelech. To renounce his claim, he took off his shoe, as was custom at the time (Ruth 4:6–8).

218.

The books of 1 and 2 Samuel tell of the introduction of kingship in Israel under the prophet Samuel. Israel's first king, Saul, was disqualified, and David became king. Three-quarters of these books are devoted to David's rise to power and to his reign. God promised David an unbroken line of successors on the throne of the kingdom.

219.

Samuel was Hannah's firstborn child (1 Samuel 1:20).

220.

After Samuel was born and weaned, his mother Hannah brought him to Shiloh to serve with Eli (1 Samuel 1:24–25).

221.

When Hannah brought Samuel to the temple to give him to the service of the Lord, she prayed, "My heart rejoiceth in the Lord, mine horn is exalted in the Lord" (1 Samuel 1:21–2:11).

222.

Besides the temple and the tabernacle, there were certain other places where people could go to speak with priests. There was a temple of the Lord at Shiloh before Solomon's temple was built (1 Samuel 1). People also met at Shechem, Bethel, Mizpah, Mounts Ebal and Gerizim, and many other places to worship God.

223.

When the Philistines took the ark of the covenant from the Israelites, they brought it to the house of Dagon. Dagon was a god of the Philistines. 1 Samuel 5:2–4 explains how the Philistines then found Dagon "fallen upon his face" before the ark on two consecutive mornings. On the second morning, "the head of Dagon and both the palms of his hands were cut off upon the threshold."

224.

When the Philistines captured the ark of the covenant, God struck them with a plague manifested by an outbreak of tumors (1 Samuel 5). Mice or rats probably transmitted it. In response, the Philistines made five golden mice and five golden tumors and sent them into Israelite territory with the ark, hoping to stop the plague.

225.

The Philistines returned the ark of the covenant to Israel by placing it in a cart and letting two unguided cows pull it to Bethshemesh (1 Samuel 6:12).

226.

When the Israelites wanted a king, Samuel warned them that a king would: make their sons be the king's charioteers, make their daughters be cooks and bakers, give the best of the fields and vineyards to his attendants, and take a tenth of the people's flocks (1 Samuel 8:10–18).

227.

Several important characters in the Bible had sons who turned out badly. The two sons of Aaron, the high priest, offered unsanctioned sacrifices (Leviticus 10). The two sons of Eli the priest abused their priestly position and were called worthless men (1 Samuel 2). Samuel's two sons took bribes and perverted justice (1 Samuel 8).

228.

Samuel's daughter-in-law gave birth to a son at a bad time in Israel's history, just after the ark of the covenant—which represented God's presence and glory—had been captured by the Philistines. Because of this, she named her son Ichabod, which means "there is no glory" or "where is the glory?"

229.

The Old Testament was written over a period of 1,000 years. The language changed over that time and occasionally needed to be updated. One example of this is in 1 Samuel 9:9: "Beforetime in Israel, when a man went to enquire of God, thus he spake, Come, and let us go to the seer: for he that is now called a Prophet was beforetime called a Seer."

230.

Shortly after Samuel anointed Saul king, Saul met a company of prophets and began to prophesy with them, surprising those around him (1 Samuel 10).

231.

Michmash was one of the war camps used during a battle between the Hebrews and the Philistines. 1 Samuel 13:5 notes that the Philistines "came up, and pitched in Michmash."

232.

Jonathan, Saul's son, won an impressive victory over the Philistines at the Pass of Michmash (1 Samuel 14), and he rightfully aspired to succeed his father as king. However, when it became clear that God had rejected his father's claim to the throne and that David would become king, he held no grudge and enthusiastically supported David.

233.

David's best friend was Jonathan, the son of King Saul. 1 Samuel 18:1 says, "the soul of Jonathan was knit with the soul of David, and Jonathan loved him as his own soul."

234.

Although Saul had called for his army to fast, Jonathan did not hear his father's command, and "put forth the end of the rod that was in his hand, and dipped it in an honeycomb, and put his hand to his mouth" (1 Samuel 14:27).

235.

The word "philistine" has come to mean uncultured or boorish in English. This is because of the mostly negative presentation in the Bible of the Philistines, who were Israel's major enemy between 1150 and 1000 B.C. The Philistine culture, however, was fairly advanced in political organization and especially in the arts.

236.

During the Early Iron Age (1150–1000 B.C.), the Philistines were Israel's major enemy and they held a monopoly of iron in Palestine. In 1 Samuel 13:19–21, it states that there were no smiths in Israel. Whoever wanted to sharpen a plowshare or another tool had to go to Philistine territory, since the Philistines did not want the Israelites to make weapons.

237.

By the early tenth century B.C., the military and technological tide had shifted in Palestine and the Philistines were no longer dominant, since Samuel, Saul, and David had subdued them. Archaeological evidence confirms this point—blacksmiths from northern Palestine were producing iron, while Philistine sites show no corresponding technological advances.

238.

Palestine is the term popularly used today to describe the land that the twelve tribes of Israel occupied during biblical times. Its name comes from the name *Philistine*, and in the Old Testament the term designates only their territory, *Philistia*. It has been a popular title for the Holy Land for 2,000 years.

239.

When Saul was tormented by an evil spirit, he was soothed by David playing on the harp (1 Samuel 16:14–23).

240.

Saul was jealous over a song that celebrated David's victory in battle: "Saul hath slain his thousands, and David his ten thousands" (1 Samuel 18:7).

241.

The fight between David and Goliath (1 Samuel 17) is one of the Old Testament's most well-known tales. But exactly how tall was Goliath? According to the Bible, the giant stood "six cubits and a span," which is more than nine feet.

242.

David had five stones in his shepherd's bag when he faced Goliath (1 Samuel 17:40).

243.

Goliath's spear is described as being "like a weaver's beam." This meant that it had a leash of cord wrapped around the spear shaft, with a loop into which he inserted his fingers. This was similar to a weaver's beam, which was a block of wood attached to a cord for separating threads. This styling would give the spear a spin, and thus a longer and truer trajectory.

244.

When David met Goliath in a one-on-one confrontation, they were engaging in a relatively uncommon "contest of champions." Each army would pick its best warrior to do battle. The winning side was determined by the results of this contest, thereby avoiding much bloodshed and death. However, when David killed Goliath, the Israelites pursued and killed many Philistines, despite the ground rules.

245.

David slew Goliath in the valley of Elah (1 Samuel 21:9).

246.

David and Jonathan made a pact that they would remain loyal to each other and each other's posterity (1 Samuel 20). After Jonathan died, David inquired about his relatives. Mephibosheth, who was crippled, was the only one left, so David took him in (2 Samuel 9).

247.

When a wealthy man named Nabal refused to help David or his men, Nabal's wife Abigail set out to prepare a feast for them and beg David's forgiveness (1 Samuel 25).

248.

Nabal was an unfortunate man. His first name means "fool," and his surname means "dog" (dogs were despised creatures in the ancient Near East). Nabal lived up to his name in his foolish dealings with David.

249.

The partridge is mentioned only twice in the Bible, once in reference to hunting it in the mountains (1 Samuel 26:20), and once in Jeremiah 17:11: "As the partridge sitteth on eggs, and hatcheth them not; so he that getteth riches, and not by right." The Hebrew word for partridge is *qore* ("one who calls"), referring to the distinctive sound it makes.

250.

Early in his reign, King Saul had tried to rid the land of mediums and wizards. However, late in life, when God no longer answered his inquiries, he used the services of a medium to inquire about his upcoming battle with the Philistines. The medium called up Samuel from the dead, who was disturbed at being called, but who prophesied Saul's death (1 Samuel 28).

251.

Saul, the king anointed by Samuel, fought his final battle on Mount Gilboa. According to 1 Samuel 31:4, Saul fell on his sword to avoid capture.

252.

The city that David captured from the Jebusites and lived in was small, about 15 acres in size. It was a walled city built on a low, elongated hill, next to which was a hidden spring. It was a significant city despite its size, and David was able to use many of the existing buildings and bureaucracy in setting up his kingdom.

253.

The Jebusites, who lived in Jerusalem before King David, were responsible for an ingenious tunnel system that brought fresh water into their city. They tunneled straight down through a hill above a spring and tapped into an underground stream. They lowered buckets and filled them from this stream and did not have to go outside the protection of the city walls.

254.

Jerusalem's water supply was its weak point, and David exploited that in capturing the city. He challenged his men to "getteth up to the gutter" which they did, either by cutting off the water supply or by going up the tunnel itself into the city (2 Samuel 5:7–9).

255.

Singing and dancing were essential components of the worship of God. The Israelites celebrated many victories with excited singing and dancing, and often women led the way. David danced a joyful and frenzied dance when the ark entered Jerusalem. Great choirs led singing in the temple courts.

256.

David's army killed 18,000 Syrians in the valley of salt (2 Samuel 8:13). Several battles were fought in this valley, including king Amaziah's victory over the Edomites (2 Kings 14:7).

257.

Ancient Near Eastern kings usually launched their military campaigns in the spring after the rainy season had ended. In Assyria, kings went out on a new campaign every year or two. Even the Bible mentions such a custom: "after the year was expired, at the time when kings go forth to battle. . . " (2 Samuel 11:1).

258.

David saw Bathsheba washing herself and summoned her to him. She was married to Uriah the Hittite. She committed adultery with King David, conceived his child, and later married him after he arranged for her husband Uriah the Hittite to be killed in battle (2 Samuel 11:1–17).

259.

Solomon was the son of David and Bathsheba (2 Samuel 12:24).

260.

Jedidiah was another name given to Solomon. It means "beloved of the Lord." After David sinned by committing adultery with Bathsheba, their child died. When their second child (Solomon) was born, David called him Jedidiah because David had been reassured that the Lord had forgiven him and still loved him, despite his sins.

261.

After being raped by her half brother, Amnon, Tamar sought protection from her full brother, Absalom. Absalom avenged Tamar's rape by arranging for Amnon to be killed (2 Samuel 13:1–29).

262.

Because Joab had ignored Absalom's summons several times, Absalom set his barley field on fire to finally capture Joab's attention (2 Samuel 14:30).

263.

Horses were common in biblical lands. They are mentioned more than 140 times in scripture. In Old Testament times, royalty held horses, and they were a symbol of human power. In Israel, kings were not to accumulate horses, but to leave military matters to God. David kept a few horses after one battle, but his son Absalom was able to capture them during his revolt against his father.

264.

King David's son Absalom died when he was hung on a tree by his hair. Absalom was riding a mule when his hair became tangled in an oak tree. His mule left, so Absalom hung from the tree by his hair (2 Samuel 18:9–10).

265.

A five-story-high rocky monolith east of the Old City of Jerusalem is called Absalom's Tomb. However, Absalom, a son of David, is not buried here. The tomb probably got its name because of a biblical reference to a monument that Absalom built for himself.

266.

Since people wore open sandals and traveled along dusty roads in Bible lands, their feet had to be washed frequently. This is mentioned several times in the Old Testament (see Genesis 18:4). Not washing one's feet was a sign of mourning (2 Samuel 19:24).

267.

Snow was (and is) rare in Bible lands, limited mainly to the high mountain ranges. Only one time is actual snowfall mentioned, but it was remembered in the same way that today we would remember outstanding storms. One of King David's warriors killed a lion "in time of snow" (2 Samuel 23:20).

268.

Under David's son Solomon, the nation began to crumble and eventually it split into two: northern Israel (ten tribes) and southern Judah (two tribes). The books of 1 and 2 Kings chronicle the fortunes of the two kingdoms. Israel had an unbroken succession of bad kings. Judah had the descendants of David and a mixture of good and bad kings. The books end with Israel annihilated and Judah under Babylonian captivity.

269.

The Bible states that David did not practice good discipline with at least one of his sons. His son Adonijah rebelliously proclaimed himself king. In 1 Kings 1:6, it says David never asked Adonijah, "Why hast thou done so?" David never held him accountable for his bad actions.

270.

After Solomon was anointed as king, there was a procession with trumpets and pipes. Adonijah learned that his brother Solomon was claiming the throne because he heard the sound of trumpets and rejoicing from the people (1 Kings 1).

271.

A "Solomonic decision" refers to a decision in a difficult judicial case that brilliantly reveals the truth or finds some middle ground. It comes from a case Solomon faced, where two women argued over the same baby. His solution was to cut the baby in half. The imposter was happy with this arrangement, but the true mother revealed herself by refusing and offering to let the other woman have the baby (1 Kings 3).

272.

In a dream, Solomon asked for wisdom in judging his people. Pleased by Solomon's request, God promised to give him not only "a wise and an understanding heart" but also "riches, and honour: so that there shall not be any among the kings like unto thee all thy days" (1 Kings 3:5–15).

273.

Solomon's wisdom exceded all men, including Ethan the Ezrahite
(1 Kings 4:29–31).

274.

Solomon created 3,000 proverbs and more than 1,000 songs
(1 Kings 4).

275.

According to the Bible, King Solomon had 700 wives and more than
300 concubines.

276.

Meat was expensive food, served to guests only on very special
occasions. Meat was common in royal palaces, however, because
kings could afford it. The normal meat ration for one day in King
Solomon's court was 10 oxen, 20 beef cows, 100 sheep, as well as
deer, gazelles, roebucks, and game birds (1 Kings 4:23).

277.

Grain was stored in storage silos and barns in the ancient world.
The Bible mentions full storehouses as being a blessing of God and
empty ones as God's curse. An impressive underground stone-
lined silo has been excavated from Megiddo, which was one of
Solomon's store cities (1 Kings 9:19).

278.

The dazzling Jerusalem Temple built by Solomon must have been a
sight to see. The materials included tons of stone blocks; boards of
cedar, olive, cypress, and algum trees; metals including gold, silver,
bronze, and iron; fabrics of purple, violet, and crimson; and beautiful
arrays of alabaster, antimony, onyx, and all kinds of colored and
precious stones.

279.

Much gold was used in Solomon's temple. The interior faces of the stonewalls were covered with fine wood and then overlaid with gold. The weight of gold coming in annually during Solomon's reign was 666 talents, or almost 50,000 pounds (1 Kings 10:14). In today's dollars, that would be worth almost $2.5 billion. Gold was so plentiful during Solomon's reign that silver was almost worthless.

280.

The temple site was so holy that the raw building materials, including the huge stone blocks for the foundations and the walls, were prepared away from the site, and then brought to be installed in place. No tools—hammers, axes, or any iron tools—were heard on location, so that even the sounds of construction could not desecrate the site.

281.

Mount Hermon is frequently referred to in the Old Testament. It is located in the north, on Lebanon's border. This snowy mountain's highest peak is about 9,232 feet (2,814 meters).

282.

Tyre, located in modern Lebanon, is mentioned frequently in the Bible. 1 Kings 9:11 tells of its king giving Solomon "cedar trees and fir trees, and with gold, according to all his desire."

283.

King Solomon used wood from the stately cedars of Lebanon in making his temple. These trees can grow to a height of 120 feet, with a circumference of up to 40 feet. The wood is fragrant, free of knots, and is not attacked by insects. Although the once plentiful trees are now rare in Lebanon, they are the country's national emblem, appearing on its national flag.

284.

The temple had two tall freestanding bronze pillars at its entrance. Both had decorated bowls (possibly fire bowls) on top. The pillars stood more than 30 feet high, and both had names: *Jachin*, meaning "(God) will establish," and *Boaz*, meaning "in him is strength." When the Babylonians destroyed the temple, they took these away with them for valuable metal.

285.

The large bronze "sea" in front of Solomon's temple had a capacity of 2,000 baths. The Hebrew *bath* was a unit of liquid measure, equal to almost six gallons (the royal bath was twice that). But the Hebrew word is not related to the English word.

286.

Worship at the temple was often messy business, since it involved killing and cutting up so many sacrificial animals, including bulls, oxen, goats, sheep, and birds. When Solomon dedicated the temple, 22,000 oxen and 120,000 sheep were sacrificed according to 1 Kings 8:63. Sacrificial altars had special channels on the sides for carrying away all the blood.

287.

Solomon had Israel's greatest chariot forces: 1,400 chariots and 12,000 horses.

288.

Solomon imported his chariot forces from Egypt and Kue in Asia Minor (1 Kings 10:26–29). He established chariot cities where he could store his forces at Hazor, Megiddo, and Gezer.

289.

Chariots were the ancient equivalents of modern-day tanks. They were very light, fast, and easily maneuverable. Chariot crews consisted of two to four men: a driver and one or more warriors, such as archers, spear throwers, and shield bearers. Chariots functioned best in flat terrain, so chariots are mentioned more often in flat Israel than in hilly Judah.

290.

After she had heard of Solomon's fame, the queen of Sheba came from her kingdom in southern Arabia or northeast Africa to test Solomon with hard questions (1 Kings 10). He impressed her with his great wisdom, knowledge, and wealth, so she honored him with huge quantities of expensive gifts.

291.

1 Kings 10:10 describes how the Queen of Sheba gifted Solomon with one hundred and twenty talents of gold, precious stones, and spices. It notes, "there came no more such abundance of spices as these which the queen of Sheba gave to king Solomon."

292.

The Bible mentions about 15 to 20 herbs and spices, not all of which can be precisely identified. Some, such as cinnamon, stacte, and frankincense, were used to make sweet-smelling incense for religious purposes. Others, like mint, dill, cumin, and garlic, were used in preparing food. Still others, such as cassia and aloes, were used for cosmetics and medicines.

293.

The prophet Ahijah the Shilonite told Jeroboam that the Lord would give him ten tribes (1 Kings 11:29–32).

294.

After Solomon's death, Jeroboam, an official who had rebelled against Solomon and then returned to foment rebellion after Solomon's death, and Rehoboam, Solomon's son, fought. The country was divided into two parts, one led by Jeroboam and one led by Rehoboam (1 Kings 12).

295.

Zimri's reign as king of Israel only lasted seven days. He died when "he went into the palace of the king's house, and burnt the king's house over him with fire" (1 Kings 16:18).

296.

King Omri paid two talents of silver for the hill of Samaria (1 Kings 16:24).

297.

The Cherith brook once provided a hiding place for the prophet Elijah. In 1 Kings 17, Elijah warns the evildoing ruler Ahab that there will be no rain for several years. To protect his prophet, God then directs Elijah to hide by this brook.

298.

When Elijah hid by the brook Cherith, God commanded the ravens to feed him, bringing him "bread and flesh" to eat (1 Kings 17:6).

299.

Mount Carmel is the only mountain range in Israel that runs to the Mediterranean Sea. Though referred to as a single mountain, it is actually a series of mountainous ridges.

300.

On Mount Carmel, Elijah challenged the priests of Baal to demonstrate that their god would light a fire on their altar (1 Kings 18:19–38).

301.

Elijah's dramatic confrontation with 400 prophets of Baal on Mount Carmel followed a long drought. Elijah was able to call down fire from heaven to ignite his offering, which "consumed the burnt sacrifice, and the wood, and the stones, and the dust, and licked up the water that was in the trench" (1 Kings 18:38).

302.

While Elijah was able to call down fire from heaven, following which it began to rain, Baal did not respond to the sacrifices of the prophets of Baal. Baal's reputation was severely damaged because he had not brought fire or changed the weather, despite his prophets' desperate pleas.

303.

Jezebel supported four hundred fifty prophets of Baal (1 Kings 18:19).

304.

Jezebel was Zidonian (1 Kings 16:31).

305.

Elijah had the prophets of Baal put to death at the Kishon brook (1 Kings 18:40).

306.

After Ahab delivered the news that Elijah had killed the prophets of Baal, Jezebel sent a messenger to Elijah threatening him with death (1 Kings 19:1–2).

307.

Three events preceded the Lord appearing to Elijah as "a still small voice." These events were a great and strong wind, then an earthquake, and then a fire (1 Kings 19:11–13).

308.

In 1 Kings 21, the Lord, speaking through the prophet Elijah, said, "The dogs shall eat Jezebel by the wall of Jezreel" (1 Kings 21:23).

309.

Elijah was taken up to heaven in a chariot of fire (2 Kings 2:11).

310.

When Elijah was taken up to heaven, he left a cloak behind for Elisha: "He took up also the mantle of Elijah that fell from him, and went back, and stood by the bank of Jordan" (2 Kings 2:13).

311.

Elisha told a widow whose husband's creditors were coming to claim her boys as slaves to ask for empty vessels from her neighbors. The widow then poured the "pot of oil" she had into the many vessels until they all were full, and she sold the oil to pay her debts and save her sons from servitude (2 Kings 4:1–7).

312.

When Elisha restored the son of the Shunammite woman to life, the first thing the boy did was sneeze: "Then he [Elisha] returned, and walked in the house to and fro; and went up, and stretched himself upon him: and the child sneezed seven times, and the child opened his eyes" (2 Kings 4:35).

313.

During a time of famine, Elisha urged his servant to put on a pot of stew for a gathering of men. A servant added a gourd from a "wild vine" to the stew, which caused the men to call the stew "death in the pot." Elisha added flour to the stew and it became edible again (2 Kings 4:38–41).

314.

Elisha told Naaman, the commander of the army of Syria, to wash in the Jordan River seven times and his leprosy would be cured (2 Kings 5:10).

315.

Joash's grandmother, Athaliah, ordered the killing of Joash along with the rest of the royal family. But her plans were spoiled when Joash's aunt "stole him from among the king's sons which were slain" (2 Kings 11:2).

316.

The Bible tells of the Assyrian king Shalmaneser's conquest of Samaria in 722 B.C., in 2 Kings 17. However, in the Assyrian annals, King Sargon II, Shalmaneser's successor, claims the credit. The problem may be resolved by assuming that Shalmaneser was still king, but his general Sargon actually took the city.

317.

Hezekiah and Josiah were among Judah's greatest kings. 2 Kings 18:5 states that Hezekiah was incomparable: Hezekiah "trusted in the Lord God of Israel, so that after him was none like him among all the kings of Judah, nor any that were before him." Josiah was incomparable also: "And like unto him there was no king before him. . . neither after him arose there any like him" (2 Kings 23:25).

318.

One of the great engineering feats recorded in the Bible was the 1,750-foot-long tunnel—through bedrock 150 feet under the City of David in Jerusalem—that was dug during King Hezekiah's reign. It provided water from a hidden spring, which would be helpful in times of siege. It was laboriously hacked out of the rock with pickaxes by two crews digging toward each other.

319.

Josiah was eight years old when he began his reign as king (2 Kings 22:1).

320.

The prophetess Huldah's husband, Shallum, was the keeper of King Josiah's wardrobe (2 Kings 22:14).

321.

King Josiah removed the "horses that the kings of Judah had given to the sun" from the entrance to the temple, and he burned their "chariots of the sun" with fire as part of his great reform movement (2 Kings 23:11).

322.

Forcing his son to pass through fire was just one of Manasseh's many wicked deeds that angered the Lord. Manasseh also "used enchantments, and dealt with familiar spirits and wizards" (2 Kings 21:1–6).

323.

King Jehoiakim reigned for a total of eleven years (2 Kings 23:36).

324.

Nebuchadnezzar was king of Babylon, and is mentioned in multiple places in the Bible.

325.

The most traumatic event for Israel in the Old Testament was the destruction of Jerusalem in 586 B.C. by the Babylonians under Nebuchadnezzar (2 Kings 25). The city was razed, the temple looted and destroyed, most of the people carried into exile, and a puppet ruler set up over the land. Even the great bronze pillars in front of the temple were carried away.

326.

The Bible records that the last king of Judah, Jehoiachin, was treated humanely while he was living in exile in Babylon (2 Kings 25:27–30). The Babylonian king freed him from prison, gave him a prestigious post among captured kings, and invited him to dine daily at the king's table. In this way, 2 Kings ends with hope for the future of God's people.

327.

As bizarre as it may be, in certain translations several verses in the Old Testament contain all letters of the alphabet but one. Ezra 7:21, for example, contains every letter except for *J*. In addition, Joshua 7:24, 1:9, 1 Chronicles 12:40, 2 Chronicles 36:10, Ezekiel 28:13, Daniel 4:37, and Haggai 1:1 contain every letter except for *Q*. And both 2 Kings 16:15 and 1 Chronicles 4:10 contain every letter except *X*.

328.

Half of the books of 1 and 2 Chronicles are copied from 1 and 2 Samuel and 1 and 2 Kings, but the author presents a very different slant. He is only interested in the fortunes of David and the kingdom of Judah (which represented David's descendants), and he consistently evaluates the nation's fortunes in terms of its trust in God.

329.

After being wounded by the Philistine's archers, King Saul asked his armor-bearer to kill him. When the armor-bearer refused, Saul fell upon his sword (1 Chronicles 10:3–4).

330.

The Levites appointed Heman (son of Joel), Asaph (son of Berechiah), and Ethan (son of Kushaiah), to be singers with instruments of music "to sound with cymbals of brass" (1 Chronicles 15:16–17, 19).

331.

A Philistine giant mentioned in 1 Chronicles 20:6 had six fingers on each hand and six toes on each foot. This phenomenon (called polydactylism) is commonly known from ancient texts and art. In an early temple in Jericho, a six-toed clay statue was found. In Assyria, a child with six fingers on the left hand was considered a good sign, but six fingers on the right hand was a sign of bad fortune.

332.

Solomon's name (Hebrew *Shelomo*) means "peace" (*shalom*), and it reflected God's promises about his kingdom. David was told that he should not build the temple in Jerusalem, because he was a man of war. Instead, God said, "A son shall be born to thee, who shall be a man of rest. . . I will give peace and quietness unto Israel in his days" (1 Chronicles 22:9).

333.

Under David's kingship, 288 men were set aside for "song in the house of the Lord, with cymbals, psalteries, and harps" (1 Chronicles 25:6).

334.

Many decisions in the Old Testament were made by drawing lots. The musicians in David's army "cast lots, ward against ward, as well the small as the great, the teacher as the student" (1 Chronicles 25:8). Nehemiah 10:34 speaks of casting lots to determine who would bring in a wood offering to the "house of our God." And Proverbs 18:18 gives a reason for the practice: "The lot causeth contentions to cease."

335.

Several biblical passages mention stalls, which were the compartments animals were kept in within stables. King Solomon had 4,000 stalls for horses and chariots (2 Chronicles 9:25). Archaeological remains of impressive stables and stalls have been recovered from Megiddo and other cities, dating to later periods in Israel's monarchy.

336.

Mount Zemaraim is notable for being near the site of a battle between Judah and Israel. According to 2 Chronicles 13, Israel's army caught Judah in an ambush, but lost the battle anyway.

337.

The ark of the covenant was created during the Exodus and accompanied the Israelites into the Promised Land. In 2 Chronicles 35:3, Josiah tells the priests, "Put the holy ark in the house which Solomon the son of David king of Israel did build." Its whereabouts were never specified after this, although Revelation 11:19 does give us a glimpse of it in God's temple in heaven.

338.

The books of Ezra and Nehemiah show the restoration of Judah after the destruction of Jerusalem and its exile in Babylon. The temple was rebuilt and Ezra and Nehemiah returned from exile to Judah to start religious and political reforms, which included rebuilding the walls of the city.

339.

King Cyrus, in the first year of his reign, allowed the Hebrew people to return to Jerusalem (Ezra 1:1–4).

340.

Ezra 1:1 does not explicitly spell out Cyrus' reasons for releasing the captives so that they could return to Jerusalem and rebuild the temple. The verse simply states, "the Lord stirred up the spirit of Cyrus king of Persia."

341.

The Bible has many genealogies, listing generation after generation seemingly endlessly. Sometimes these genealogies are not all-inclusive, however. For instance, a list of Aaron's descendants in Ezra 7:1–5 omits six people who are found in the parallel list in 1 Chronicles 6:3–14.

342.

The prophet Ezra proclaimed a fast at the Ahava River (Ezra 8:21).

343.

In the Old Testament, the first 17 books (Genesis through Esther) are in essentially chronological order, beginning with creation and ending with the Jews in exile at the end of the Old Testament period. Other books are not grouped chronologically. The prophetic books are arranged with the three longest books first. Most of the prophets fit chronologically into the time period covered by 1 and 2 Kings.

344.

India is mentioned twice in the Bible. Esther 1:1 mentions a ruler named Ahasuerus, who ruled "from India even unto Ethiopia." Esther 8:9 also mentions provinces of India.

345.

When Esther's parents died, an older cousin named Mordecai took her in and raised her as his own daughter (Esther 2:7).

346.

After Vashti disobeyed King Ahasuerus' command to appear before his royal feast, she was deposed as queen (Esther 1:9–19).

347.

In the book of Esther, no one could approach the king if they had not been summoned. If they did, they would only be spared death if the king held out a golden scepter. Xerxes did so to spare Esther's life when she came before him.

348.

After Vashti was removed as queen, King Ahasuerus married Esther, "And the king loved Esther above all the women, and she obtained grace and favour in his sight more than all the virgins; so that he set the royal crown upon her head, and made her queen instead of Vashti" (Esther 2:17).

349.

The longest verse in the Bible is Esther 8:9.

350.

Many different types of merchants produced products for sale, which were often sold at the city gate. In larger cities, tradespeople of the same trade lived in the same neighborhood. So there would be the potters' section of town, the food market, the cheese makers' valley, and so on. Nehemiah mentions the "tower of the furnaces," which suggests bakeries clustered together (Nehemiah 3:11).

351.

The book of Job is one of the world's classics on the question of human suffering. Job, an innocent man who feared God, is put through much suffering. Through this, Job passionately questions God but he never abandons belief in God. After a direct encounter with God, Job's questions cease and his fortunes are fully restored.

352.

Job had seven sons and three daughters (Job 1:1–2).

353.

Job 28 contains a majestic poem about wisdom. It states that wisdom is not to be found in the deepest sea, nor can it be bought for gold, nor can any animal or human being know it on its own. Only "God understandeth the way thereof, and he knoweth the place thereof" (verse 23). God reveals wisdom to humans.

354.

The ostrich was common in biblical lands, but today it is extinct there. It was used for food and for its feathers, and it is occasionally depicted in the art of Egypt and Assyria. Ostriches are described in considerable detail in Job 39:13–18, where their reputation for cruelty and stupidity is mentioned, as well as their blinding speed.

355.

The Hebrew word *behemoth* is a rare word for "beasts." In Job 40:15, it refers to a large animal, probably the hippopotamus. The modern-day meaning of something large takes its meaning from this passage.

356.

The longest book in the Bible is Psalms, with an impressive 150 chapters.

357.

The 150 psalms in the Psalter formed a hymnbook of sorts for Israel. These hymns cover the range of human emotion, from ecstatic joy to deepest despair. They have taught Christians how to sing and pray, and also convey truths about God and everyday faith and life.

358.

A well-written essay usually states its objective at the beginning. Some biblical psalms, however, make their main point halfway through.

359.

Winnowing is throwing the threshed grain into the air so the wind blows away the straw (or chaff). The heavier grains fall to the ground and are saved, after which the grain is ready for storing or selling. Psalm 1 speaks of the insignificance of the wicked in God's sight as "like the chaff which the wind driveth away."

360.

Mount Zion is mentioned in multiple places in the Bible. It is located in Jerusalem, and (more aptly) described as a hill, as in Psalm 2:6: "Yet have I set my king upon my holy hill of Zion." It has been the site of fortifications and settlements for centuries.

361.

Psalm 3 begins: "Lord, how are they increased that trouble me! Many are they that rise up against me." The psalm was written by David when he was fleeing from Absalom.

362.

Some psalms appear more than once in the Bible. David's song of praise when God delivered him from the hands of Saul appears as 2 Samuel 22 and also as Psalm 18. The psalm beginning, "The fool hath said in his heart, There is no God," appears both as Psalm 14 and 53.

363.

Shepherds had two important tools in Bible times: a rod and a staff. The staff was a long pole, sometimes bent at the end, for prodding and guiding sheep. The rod was a shorter club used to defend against predators. Both appear in the well-known Shepherd's Psalm: "Thy rod and thy staff they comfort me" (Psalm 23:4).

364.

Hebrew has some 12 different words for sheep, such as ram, ewe, and flock. This undoubtedly reflects the important place sheep had in Israelite life and economy in Old Testament times. In the Bible, sheep are symbolically seen as innocent, sacrificial animals. Psalm 23 is one of the best-known passages to reference the animal: "The Lord is my shepherd; I shall not want" (verse 1).

365.

Psalm 32 is a beautiful reflection on the joys of having one's sins forgiven. It uses no fewer than four words for sin in its opening lines: "Blessed is he whose *transgression* is forgiven, whose *sin* is covered. Blessed is the man unto whom the Lord *imputeth* not iniquity, and in whose spirit there is no *guile*." The variety of terms used creates the solid assurance that whatever the sin, it is covered and forgiven.

366.

Several different words for deer are found in the Bible. The "hart" is probably the roe deer. The male of the species weighs up to 300 pounds and has six-pronged antlers. It is not well suited for desert living, which is reflected in Psalm 42:1: "As the hart panteth after the water brooks. . . " The Bible usually mentions deer metaphorically, referring often to their graceful running and leaping abilities.

367.

Psalm 51 begins: "Have mercy upon me, O God, according to thy lovingkindness." The psalm was written by David after Nathan had rebuked him for committing adultery with Bathsheba and arranging Uriah's death. The psalm continues, "According unto the multitude of thy tender mercies blot out my transgressions. Wash me thoroughly from mine iniquity, and cleanse me from my sin."

368.

Hyperbole, or exaggeration, is a common poetic device. In describing his troubles, one psalmist says, "I sink in deep mire, where there is no standing: I have come into deep waters, where the floods overflow me" (Psalm 69:2). It is comical to imagine the poet literally holding a scroll and pen above the water as he sinks out of sight!

369.

Besides the 150 psalms in the biblical Psalter, the Bible has many other psalms scattered throughout other books. Famous examples include psalms in Exodus 15 (Moses and Miriam's Song of the Sea), Deuteronomy 32 (Moses' song), Judges 5 (Deborah and Barak's victory song), 1 Samuel 2 (Hannah's song of praise), 2 Samuel 1 (David's lament), Jonah 2 (Jonah's prayer of thanksgiving), and Habakkuk 3 (Habakkuk's song of praise).

370.

Some psalms were composed in much the same way that modern church prayer books are, by stringing together different portions of scripture to form new compositions. Psalm 108 is made up entirely of parts of Psalm 57 and 60, and the lengthy hymn of thanksgiving when the ark reached Jerusalem found in 1 Chronicles 16 is composed of poetry found in three psalms: 96, 105, and 106.

371.

Several women in the Old Testament are described as childless at some point: Sarah, Rebekah, Rachel (all wives of the patriarchs), and Samson's mother, Hannah. In biblical times, being childless was a woman's greatest misfortune. However, each of these women was eventually given a child in the tradition expressed in Psalm 113:9: "He maketh the barren woman to keep house, and to be a joyful mother of children."

372.

The Bible's shortest chapter, Psalms 117, comes just two chapters before its longest chapter. It is a beautiful little gem, a burst of praise to God, urging people to praise God for his goodness and faithfulness. It is only two verses long!

373.

The Bible mentions bees a number of times. Twice the swarming habits of honeybees are mentioned: Psalm 118:12 says that "[The nations] compassed me about like bees," while Deuteronomy 1:44 mentions the Amorites chasing the Israelites like bees. The Hebrew word for "bee" is *deborah*.

374.

The longest chapter in the Bible is Psalm 119 (a dizzying 176 verses).

375.

The book of Proverbs is one of the most practical books in the Bible, with its common-sense approach to life. This is captured in hundreds of short, pithy sayings (proverbs) about how to live well in all dimensions, with God and our neighbors.

376.

Wisdom in the biblical sense refers to knowing how to live life well, in all its dimensions, including relationships with God and one's fellow human beings. The three "wisdom" books in the Bible are Job, Proverbs, and Ecclesiastes. The book of Proverbs begins by stating that "The fear of the Lord is the beginning of knowledge: but fools despise wisdom and instruction" (Proverbs 1:7).

377.

Among the proverbs of Agur in Proverbs 30 is a list of four things he does not understand: "the way of an eagle in the air; the way of a serpent upon a rock; the way of a ship in the midst of the sea; and the way of a man with a maid" (verse 19).

378.

The book of Ecclesiastes is written by someone who has tried everything in search for meaning in life, but comes up empty. It is full of frustration, even cynicism, but the book ends by affirming that life has meaning when lived in the right relation with God. It is the closest piece of writing in the Bible to what the Greeks called philosophy.

379.

The author of Ecclesiastes uses the phrase "under the sun" more than 25 times as he expresses weariness with life. In his search for fulfillment, he discovers that: "The thing that hath been, it is that which shall be; and that which is done is that which shall be done: and there is no new thing under the sun" (Ecclesiastes 1:9). He concludes that the search for something new is misguided, that fulfillment comes in fearing God.

380.

The author of Ecclesiastes voiced the complaints of endless generations of students when he said, "Of making many books there is no end; and much study is a weariness of the flesh" (Ecclesiastes 12:12). His point was that fearing God and pleasing him are what bring true fulfillment.

381.

In the rich love poetry of the Song of Solomon, a beloved woman compares herself to the "rose of Sharon" (2:1). What was this beautiful flower? It was actually not a rose, but probably a tulip of some kind, either *Tulipa montana* or the *Tulipa sharonensis*, which grows deep red among the grasses on the Plain of Sharon.

382.

Foxes were well known in biblical lands. Their fondness for grapes is mentioned in Song of Solomon 2:15, and Judges 15:4–5 describes how Samson caught 300 foxes, tied them together with lighted torches between their tails, and sent them into the Philistines' fields.

383.

Two books in the Bible do not mention God even once: the love poetry of the Song of Solomon, and the book of Esther, which tells of life and success under Persian rule.

384.

The Song of Solomon ends with one of the lovers urging the other to "Make haste, my beloved, and be thou like to a roe or to a young hart upon the mountains of spices" (Song of Solomon 8:14).

385.

The book of Isaiah is arguably the greatest of the prophetic books. Its scope is all encompassing. The book ranges from dramatic criticisms of wicked Judah to tender assurances of God's love and restoration to visions of the new heavens and the new earth.

386.

The prophet Isaiah was the son of Amoz (2 Kings 19:20).

387.

The term Mount Zion originally referred to the low hill of Jerusalem on which King David built his early city. Later, it was transferred to a higher hill to the west. It came to symbolize the capital of God's kingdom, and Isaiah and Micah spoke of Mount Zion as ultimately being established "in the top of the mountains. . . exalted above the hills" (Isaiah 2:2; Micah 4:1).

388.

Isaiah prophesied that the Lord would punish the kings of the earth by gathering them together as prisoners in a pit (Isaiah 24:21–22).

389.

Do crocodiles appear in scripture? Maybe. Old Testament poetry references a creature named Leviathan. Isaiah calls it "the piercing serpent. . . the dragon that is in the sea" (27:1). Job says, "His teeth are terrible round about. His scales are his pride" (41:14–15). These descriptions lead many scholars to believe that Leviathan is the crocodile of the Nile.

390.

A hot south and east wind blows across Egypt and Palestine during the months of May and October. It fills the air with dust and often lasts three days or more. The Bible mentions this wind many times as a symbol of God's wrath. Isaiah describes how God removed his people into exile: "He stayeth his rough wind in the day of the east wind" (Isaiah 27:8).

391.

The crane is a beautiful, large wading bird, with long neck, legs, and bill, similar to a heron. It is mentioned twice in the Bible. Isaiah 38:14 mentions its noisy call, and Jeremiah 8:7 describes its regular migrating habits.

392.

Eagles are mentioned more often than any bird of prey in the Bible. They are impressive for their great size, strength, speed, and soaring abilities. They are usually mentioned using stirring words, like in Isaiah 40:31: "But they that wait upon the Lord shall renew their strength; they shall mount up with wings as eagles."

393.

Isaiah 43:24 mentions sweet cane. A wild cane is found throughout Palestine, but most scholars think this refers to the sugarcane. Honey was the most important sweetener in Old Testament times, but this cane was probably chewed or used to sweeten drinks and food.

394.

The prophet Isaiah painted an exquisite word picture of comfort for Jerusalem when he stated: "How beautiful upon the mountains are the feet of him that bringeth good tidings, that publisheth peace; that bringeth good tidings of good, that publisheth salvation; that saith unto Zion, Thy God reigneth!" (Isaiah 52:7). The focus on the feet of messengers adds to the impact of the uplifting message.

395.

The prophet Jeremiah revealed his personal passions more than any other prophet. He wept bitterly over the sins of his people and argued bitterly with God for sending him as a prophet. He was vigorously opposed by false prophets and suffered much for his stand. Lamentations also includes passionate laments over the destruction of Jerusalem, traditionally ascribed to Jeremiah.

396.

Although Psalms has the most chapters of any book in the Bible (150), the book of Jeremiah (with a mere 52 chapters) has the most words. Jeremiah was a passionate prophet, pouring out his heart at great length and with great emotion to God.

397.

God called Jeremiah a prophet before he was even born. God says, "Before I formed thee in the belly I knew thee; and before thou camest forth out of the womb I sanctified thee, and I ordained thee a prophet unto the nations" (Jeremiah 1:5).

398.

When God called Jeremiah to prophesy, Jeremiah responded, "I am a child" (Jeremiah 1:6).

399.

God told Jeremiah never to marry or have children, since conditions would soon become so awful in the land that children would die in great numbers and not be mourned or buried. This was because of the evil that had infested the land.

400.

The prophet Jeremiah speaks of professional women mourners who could be summoned in order to "take up a wailing for us." This skill was passed on to their daughters and even their neighbors (Jeremiah 9:17–20). But the Bible forbade anything too excessive: "Ye shall not cut yourselves, nor make any baldness between your eyes for the dead" (Deuteronomy 14:1). Israel's neighbors practiced these self-destructive customs.

401.

A dramatic confrontation of a true and false prophet occurred between Jeremiah and Hananiah (Jeremiah 28). Hananiah claimed to speak for God, and he offered a soothing message to the people, while Jeremiah's message was much harsher. Jeremiah was vindicated when he correctly foretold Hananiah's imminent death.

402.

The Hinnom valley just outside of Jerusalem is condemned several times in the Old Testament as a place of child sacrifice. Jeremiah 32:35 says, "And they built the high places of Baal, which are in the valley of the son of Hinnom, to cause their sons and their daughters to pass through the fire unto Molech."

403.

Book burning isn't just a modern-day occurrence. The Bible mentions that King Jehoiakim of Judah burned the book of Jeremiah in the fire that was on the hearth, "until all the roll was consumed in the fire" (Jeremiah 36:23).

404.

When Jeremiah was thrown in a cistern, a royal official pleaded with the king for his life and was allowed to save him. Ebedmelech, an Ethiopian palace official, interceded with the king on Jeremiah's behalf and was directed to save Jeremiah (Jeremiah 38).

405.

Jeremiah emphasized strongly that the Jews should not resist the Babylonians, since they were God's instrument to punish Judah's sins. Many in Jerusalem, however, did not like this counsel. They accused Jeremiah of being a traitor, saying, "He weakeneth the hands of the men of war that remain in this city. . . This man seeketh not the welfare of this people, but the hurt" (Jeremiah 38:4).

406.

The book of Ezekiel contains many strange visions and strange actions. His message was to those in Babylonian exile, helping them to make sense of their punishment and pointing them to a way of restoration. Along with Jeremiah, he emphasized the concept of each individual's responsibility for his or her own sin, a concept that had been forgotten in Judah. His book ends with a great vision of the ideal temple.

407.

Ezekiel had a glittering vision about four shining manlike creatures that were accompanied by four wheels (Ezekiel 1). The creatures each had four wings and four faces: a man, a lion, an ox, and an eagle. The wheels did not turn, but they had eyes in them, and they flew wherever the creatures flew. The vision portrayed God's majesty in vivid terms.

408.

Ezekiel 2:8–3:3 describes the prophet eating a scroll that contains God's words as a symbol of internalizing them. Ezekiel calls the scroll "as sweet as honey," which echoes the words of Psalm 119:103: "How sweet are thy words unto my taste! Yea, sweeter than honey to my mouth!"

409.

God took Ezekiel's wife, the "desire of his eyes," from him, but Ezekiel was instructed not to mourn, weep, or make any public display for her. This was to foreshadow God's destruction of the temple, which Judah was not to mourn, since Judah had so greatly profaned it and its worship.

410.

Ezekiel prophesied that God would cause many nations to attack Tyrus, destroy its walls, and break down its towers (Ezekiel 26:2–4).

411.

The book of Daniel contains an equal mixture of stories about Daniel and his friends in exile—such as Daniel in the lion's den or his three friends (Shadrach, Meshach, and Abednego) in the fiery furnace—and of visions about the future. The common thread between both parts of the book is the idea of God's control of the world's empires and his vindication of his people.

412.

In exile at the court of Nebuchadnezzar in Babylon, Daniel and his companions proposed to eat and drink "pulse and water" instead of partaking of the royal food and wine. Pulse means "legumes" (Daniel 1:12).

413.

Interpretation of dreams was an important means of discerning the will of God in biblical times. Every ancient king retained court wise men to interpret dreams. Joseph and Daniel are the best-known dream interpreters in the Bible. Daniel was even required to tell the Babylonian king what the king had dreamed, and then interpret it for him.

414.

King Nebuchadnezzar dreamed of a great statue made of gold, brass, iron, and clay, which was destroyed by a stone that then became a mountain. Daniel interpreted it for him: the elements of the statue represented different kingdoms that would eventually be replaced by God's kingdom (Daniel 2).

415.

The penalty for not worshipping the golden statue that Nebuchadnezzar had raised whenever "ye hear the sound of the cornet, flute, harp, sackbut, psaltery, dulcimer, and all kinds of musick" was to be thrown in a fiery furnace (Daniel 3:4–6).

416.

King Nebuchadnezzar threw Shadrach, Meshach, and Abednego into a fiery furnace for their refusal to serve his gods or worship the golden image he set up (Daniel 3:14–20).

417.

The book of Daniel tells of King Nebuchadnezzar's being humbled by God. He was driven away from Babylon and lived with the beasts of the field. "His body was wet with the dew of heaven, till his hair were grown like eagles' feathers, and his nails like birds' claws" (Daniel 4:33).

418.

King Nebuchadnezzar went insane, was driven from men, and ate grass "as oxen" (Daniel 4:33).

419.

Babylonian king Belshazzar saw a hand writing words on the wall. The cryptic message said, *"Mene, Mene, Tekel, Upharsin,"* and only Daniel was able to interpret the writing: *numbered, numbered, weighed, divided*. Belshazzar's days were numbered, his kingdom wasn't worth its weight, so it would be divided and given to the Medes and Persians (Daniel 5:12–28).

420.

In biblical times, people prayed at any time of the day or night. There were formal prayers for morning and evening services in the temple. Daniel prayed three times a day in his bedroom. And Nehemiah prayed while he was working: Several times he uttered quick, impromptu prayers under his breath when a crisis arose.

421.

A lion's den is mentioned in the story of Daniel, who was thrown into one when he refused to stop praying toward Jerusalem (Daniel 6:16–24). When he was vindicated, his false accusers and their families were themselves thrown in the den and devoured by lions. This practice was not known otherwise in the ancient Near East, but Job 38:39–40 does speak of lions crouching in their dens.

422.

"The Ancient of Days" is a title given to God in Daniel 7, describing the last judgment. God is described as enthroned on a fiery throne, with snow-white clothing and hair white like pure wool. It is an elegant description for an old man, and it emphasizes God's eternal nature as it contrasts with the earthly kingdoms described in the chapter.

423.

In one of Daniel's visions, he saw an accurate picture of Alexander the Great and his empire. He reported seeing a goat with "a notable horn between his eyes. . . The he goat waxed very great; and when he was strong, the great horn was broken; and for it came up four notable ones toward the four winds of heaven" (Daniel 8:5–8).

424.

The book of Daniel contains explicit words about the book's focus: Much of it was not for the present, but for a future time. Daniel was instructed in a vision to "shut thou up the vision; for it shall be for many days" (Daniel 8:26) and to "seal the book, even to the time of the end" (Daniel 12:4).

425.

There are twelve "minor prophets" that make up the final twelve books of the Old Testament (Hosea 1:1–Malachi 4:6).

426.

The Lord instructed Hosea to take a wife and children of whoredoms because "the land hath committed great whoredom, departing from the Lord" (Hosea 1:2).

427.

The prophet Hosea's unfaithful wife was named Gomer (Hosea 1:2–3).

428.

The short book of Joel focuses on the concept of the "Day of the Lord." This sometimes refers to God's immediate judgment on nations that oppressed others (such as in a great locust plague), and sometimes refers to God's judgment of all nations at the end of time.

429.

The eighth plague on Egypt was an incredible swarm of locusts, and the books of Joel and Revelation depict locusts as God's instruments of judgment. Even in modern times, swarms of locusts have darkened the skies and devastated areas up to 400 square miles.

430.

Sometimes word links between adjacent books of the Bible can be seen, which probably accounts for their being placed together. The following phrase occurs near the end of the book of Joel: "The Lord also shall roar out of Zion, and utter his voice from Jerusalem" (Joel 3:16). The next book, Amos, begins with the same phrase (Amos 1:2).

431.

More than any prophet, Amos spoke out against social evils, such as abuse of power, oppression of the poor, dishonest dealings, and insincere religious ritual. He even spoke out against the life of leisure, and the many possessions and summer homes of the wealthy. These luxuries blinded the people to the very real needs around them.

432.

The prophet Amos speaks of God roaring like a lion from Jerusalem because he is angry at the nation of Israel, and the blast of his roar causing the top of Mount Carmel to wither. Mount Carmel is a lush, wooded mountain more than 70 miles north of Jerusalem. God's breath not only reaches Carmel, but it scorches the shepherd's pastures along the way (Amos 1:2).

433.

The altar of burnt offering had four horns (like the pointed horns of an animal such as a bull), one on each corner. These were considered the ultimate place of refuge and security. When the prophet Amos announced that even the horns of the altar at Bethel would be cut off, he was saying that there was no more escape for that wicked city (Amos 3:14).

434.

Fish and fishing are mentioned symbolically many times in the Bible. Usually the imagery has to do with catching fish, whether with nets or otherwise. An example is Amos' jarring prophecy about Samaria's doom: "He will take you away with hooks, and your posterity with fishhooks" (Amos 4:2).

435.

The prophet Amos, like most of the prophets, often used picturesque language to make his point. In one passage, to illustrate that God had used famine to try to jolt Israel out of its spiritual lethargy, he says that God gave Israel "cleanness of teeth" (Amos 4:6). This is not a reference to personal hygiene, but instead means they had no food to get between their teeth.

436.

The prophet Amos said, "Jeroboam shall die by the sword, and Israel shall surely be led away captive out of their own land" (Amos 7:11).

437.

The prophet Amos was a "gatherer of sycamore fruit" by profession (Amos 7:14). The figs of the sycamore tree require cutting open with a knifepoint at a certain stage to help in the ripening process, and this is what Amos did.

438.

When the prophet Amos protested that he was not a prophet nor a prophet's son (Amos 7:14), he meant that he had not been raised or trained as a prophet, and he did not make his living prophesying. Rather, he had his own profession, and he was prophesying only because God had sent him on a special mission.

439.

The Bible mentions eclipses several times, as prophetic signs of God's judgment. Amos 8:9 states, "I will cause the sun to go down at noon, and I will darken the earth in the clear day." Joel 2:31 says, "The sun shall be turned into darkness, and the moon into blood." Lunar eclipses do indeed look red at times, due to refraction of the sun's light.

440.

The prophet Amos gives a startlingly vivid picture of what conditions would soon be like in Israel because of its rejection of the Lord: "I will send a famine in the land, not a famine of bread, nor a thirst for water, but of hearing the words of the Lord: And they shall wander from sea to sea, and from the north even to the east, they shall run to and fro to seek the word of the Lord, and shall not find it" (Amos 8:11–12).

441.

The Book of Obadiah is the shortest book in the Old Testament. It's a brief but concentrated blast of condemnation at Judah's neighbor Edom, located southeast of the Dead Sea. Edom had rejoiced at Jerusalem's downfall, and this book speaks about that.

442.

The message of the book of Jonah is often obscured by discussions about the fish that swallowed the prophet. It is a wonderful book about God's concern for all people, not just his chosen people. Jonah was sent to Nineveh, the capital of the world's largest empire, to urge its people to repent, and they did.

443.

When asked to preach God's message in Nineveh, Jonah boarded a ship headed to Tarshish to flee from the Lord (Jonah 1:1–3).

444.

Jonah took passage on a ship—ultimately ending up in a fish's belly for three days—to avoid God's command to "go to Nineveh, that great city, and cry against it; for their wickedness is come up before me" (Jonah 1:2).

445.

The book of Jonah states that Jonah took a ship going to Tarshish rather than go to Nineveh, as God had commanded him. Tarshish was either part of the island of Sardinia (off the coast of Italy) or a region in far-off Spain. It is obvious that Jonah's intent was to go as far away from Nineveh as he could.

446.

While Jonah waited to see what would happen to Nineveh, God provided him a vine to shade him (Jonah 4:6).

447.

Micah fits well the stereotype of a biblical prophet, speaking out against both social and spiritual evils, and also looking into the future and speaking of the restoration of God's people. He predicted that the Messiah would come from Bethlehem, and he summarized well the duties of God's people: "And what doth the Lord require of thee, but to do justly, and to love mercy, and to walk humbly with thy God" (Micah 6:8).

448.

The prophet Zechariah saw a man on the red horse standing among the myrtle trees in his vision (Zechariah 1:8).

449.

The land of Hadrach is only mentioned once in the Bible. It appears in Zechariah 9:1: "The burden of the word of the Lord in the land of Hadrach, and Damascus shall be the rest thereof."

450.

Several passages in the Old Testament speak of a king riding on a donkey. This is most striking in Zechariah 9:9, where it is prophesied that a king comes triumphant and victorious yet riding humbly on a donkey (and chariots and war horses are mentioned in the next verse). Jesus' entrance into Jerusalem fulfilled this prophecy (Matthew 21:5).

451.

Herod the Great ruled Israel in the time of Christ. He was a vicious man, and ordered his soldiers to kill all of the infant boys in Bethlehem to keep Jesus from becoming king.

452.

King Herod was a ruthless and unpopular ruler who was put in power by the Romans. He executed dozens of political rivals, including a favorite wife and two of his own sons.

453.

Although Jerusalem had been destroyed and rebuilt about five centuries before Christ, King Herod undertook a massive public works project. The improvements included the temple, a fortress, viaducts to bring water, public monuments, and an amphitheater, as well as palaces and citadels.

454.

King Herod fortified Jerusalem by building huge walls and high towers around the city. A three-tower complex defended his palace. The base of one of these towers, named Phasael's Tower, can still be seen today. It is an impressive 60-foot cube, and is popularly, but erroneously, known as David's Tower. It was 150 feet high.

455.

The Temple hill was sloped on all sides, so Herod had large terraces constructed to enlarge the platform. The Temple Mount measured roughly 984 feet by 1,640 feet (300 meters by 500 meters), and in some places the height of the walls reached a little over 164 feet (50 meters)!

456.

In 23 B.C., King Herod built a spectacular palace-fortress complex for himself in the wilderness southeast of Jerusalem. A 90-foot-high cylindrical double wall was constructed around the top of a natural hill, and then a sloping fill of earth and gravel added around it, partially burying the wall. This created an impregnable cone-shaped mountain that is visible from Jerusalem, eight miles away.

457.

Herod's Herodium, 200 feet wide, was a luxurious place. Seven stories of living rooms, storage areas, and cisterns were built, including a complete Roman bathhouse and a beautiful open courtyard. It was the third largest palace in the Roman world, and by far the most luxurious in Israel.

458.

In 4 B.C., two babies were born, cousins named John and Jesus. The lives of these cousins shared several similarities. Both sets of parents were visited by angels and were told that their child would do great things. Both men would also die violently in their early 30s.

459.

Angels are regularly described in the Bible as beings of light. Sometimes they look like men in bright clothing. And people are usually terrified to see them: The angel Gabriel told both Zacharias and Mary not to be afraid of him.

460.

Gabriel is mentioned only four times in the Bible. Twice he appeared to Daniel to teach him things beyond his comprehension. In the New Testament, Gabriel announced to Zacharias the priest the coming birth of his son, John the Baptist, and he announced to Mary the coming birth of Jesus. *Gabriel* means "God is mighty" or "mighty man of God."

461.

When an elderly priest named Zacharias was chosen to burn incense in the temple, the angel Gabriel appeared to tell him that he and his wife would have a son. The son, Jesus' cousin, would be John the Baptist. He would "make ready a people prepared for the Lord" (Luke 1:17). Zacharias would not believe it, and the angel took his voice away. He didn't speak again until John was born.

462.

Elizabeth was the mother of John the Baptist, descended from "the daughters of Aaron" (Luke 1:5). Her name was the same as Aaron's wife's (Exodus 6:23); its Hebrew form means "my God is (my) oath" (or "one who worships God").

463.

When Mary and Elizabeth met, and the baby leapt in Elizabeth's womb, Mary proclaimed, "My soul doth magnify the Lord, and my spirit hath rejoiced in God my Saviour" (Luke 1:41–56).

464.

A firstborn son generally received the name of his grandfather. People were surprised when the mother of John the Baptist insisted his name was John. "There is none of thy kindred that is called by this name," they said (Luke 1:61). The name means "God is gracious."

465.

Angels are not always named in biblical accounts, but it was Gabriel who announced Christ's birth to Mary. He is also assumed to be the angel who announced the birth of Christ to the shepherds and guarded the holy family on its flight to Egypt.

466.

The angel Gabriel appeared to Mary to tell her she was chosen to give birth to the Son of God (Luke 1:26–32). The angel said, "The Holy Ghost shall come upon thee," and Mary replied, "Be it unto me according to thy word" (1:35, 38). The Virgin Birth is mentioned by both Luke and Matthew, and has been a central belief since the earliest days of the Church.

467.

At the time there were different greetings between strangers, between men, between women, and between married people or adults and children. We are told Mary was confused when the angel appeared and said, "Hail, thou that art highly favoured, the Lord is with thee." She "cast in her mind what manner of salutation this should be" because no one she knew had ever used such a greeting (Luke 1:26–29).

468.

An agreement between families was celebrated and the groom began an engagement by saying, "This is my wife and I her husband, from today and forever." It was after this moment had happened that Joseph considered "putting away" (divorcing) his pregnant fiancée Mary, but an angel told him not to. (See Matthew 1:18–20.)

469.

During the time of Jesus' birth, Caesar Augustus sent out a decree that all people should be registered for taxes (Luke 2:1–3).

470.

When the Roman emperor required everyone to be registered for tax purposes, he had no idea that this would move Mary and Joseph from their home in Nazareth to Bethlehem—just in time for Jesus to be born in their ancient tribal home. Proverbs 21:1 says, "The king's heart is in the hand of the Lord."

471.

Although we picture Mary traveling by donkey, Luke never identifies her means of transportation. Since Joseph was an established tradesman, they could have traveled in a carriage. It was also possible to rent a carriage or wagon in one town and leave it in another.

472.

The census forms Joseph would have completed when he traveled to Bethlehem with Mary are well documented. They were sworn statements that included names, ages, and physical descriptions, including any distinguishing features such as scars. Birth certificates required the same information.

473.

Bethlehem means "house of bread." It is mentioned several times in the Old Testament, most prominently as the city where David was from, but its major importance was as Jesus' birthplace. It is about five miles south of Jerusalem and overlooked an ancient highway from Hebron to Egypt.

474.

Bethlehem was not the sleepy little village we often imagine. It was on a well-known trade route and only three miles from one of Herod's palaces. Travelers had to go through Bethlehem en route to the palace, which was the center of administration for places south of Jerusalem.

475.

The "inn" in Luke 2 is translated from a word that could refer to a guest room adjoining a private home, in this case perhaps some relative of Joseph or Mary. Because the room was already occupied, the pair had to lodge in the stable. This would explain the "house" they were living in when visited by the magi (Matthew 2:11).

476.

The Gospel of Luke mentions the manger into which Jesus was laid when he was born (Luke 2:7). Most scholars think this was a feeding trough for cattle. Excavations at Megiddo and Lachish, towns of the Old Testament period, have uncovered stone feeding troughs of this type.

477.

The Bible records several instances in which God grants someone a child under miraculous circumstances: Sarah had Isaac at 90. Although they were barren, he gave Samuel to Hannah, Jacob and Esau to Rebekah, Joseph to Rachel, and John the Baptist to Elizabeth. Mary, a virgin, was the mother of Jesus.

478.

Mary was about 13 or 14 when she had Jesus. She would not have gone to school or been taught to read or write. Her days would have been spent mostly fetching water, tending the fire, or grinding grain. She was from a religious family, however, and therefore knew about Old Testament teachings regarding the Messiah.

479.

The name Jesus (in Greek *Iesous*) is related to the Hebrew name *Yeshua*, which means "one who saves" or "Yahweh saves." It can also be translated as *Joshua*.

480.

An angel told Joseph to name Mary's son Jesus, "for he shall save his people from their sins" (Matthew 1:21).

481.

Christ was not part of the name that Mary gave Jesus. The term is a title, and it comes from the Greek word for "messiah" (*christos*). Thus, Jesus was often referred to as "the Christ" (the Messiah).

482.

Our word *Messiah* comes from the Hebrew word *mashiach*, which means "anointed one." In the New Testament the word is used about 500 times to refer to Jesus, who said he came to set up a spiritual kingdom.

483.

In the Old Testament, kings were anointed into their office; so any number of kings could be called messiahs. The New Testament presents Jesus as the Messiah, the one ultimate and perfect king.

484.

One of the most famous prophecies about the Messiah is found in Isaiah 7:14, where a virgin is to conceive and bear a son named Immanuel. This name is *Imma-nu-el* in Hebrew, literally translated it means "with us (is) God." Matthew 1:23 quotes this as having been fulfilled in Jesus.

485.

Matthew said Jesus would be called a Nazarene, fulfilling an Old Testament prophecy (Matthew 2:23). This does not refer to his childhood in Nazareth, however. This likely refers to the Hebrew word *netzer*, meaning branch. Isaiah 11:1 says "And there shall come forth a rod out of the stem of Jesse, and a Branch [*netzer*] shall grow out of his roots."

486.

Jesus' last name wasn't "Christ." Normally he would have gone by Joshua ben Joseph, and he was probably known that way in Nazareth. Jesus' ancestry can be traced back to King David on both sides of his family, through Joseph in Matthew's Gospel and through Mary in Luke's.

487.

When speaking of the genealogy of Jesus, the number 14 has significance. Matthew 1:17 says, "So all the generations from Abraham to David are fourteen generations; and from David until the carrying away into Babylon are fourteen generations; and from the carrying away into Babylon unto Christ are fourteen generations."

488.

Unlike most biblical genealogies, Matthew's genealogy of Jesus includes female descendants: Rahab, Ruth, Bathsheba, Tamar, and Jesus' mother, Mary. Tamar pretended to be a prostitute, Rahab was a prostitute, Bathsheba was an adulteress, and Mary, his mother, was probably considered an unwed mother. God often uses and blesses those whom others look down upon.

489.

Genesis 49:10 says that a king will come from Judah and that all the nations will obey him. Jesus, of course, was from this tribe, and Bible scholars say this is only one of many promises about him. As many as 250 references are made to Jesus in the books of the Old Testament, written before he was born.

490.

The angel that announced the birth of Christ to the shepherds was accompanied by "the glory of the Lord," appearing as a great light. Glory as light was known as *Shekinah*, indicating the presence of God. (See Numbers 14:21 and Exodus 33:18–22.)

491.

Why were shepherds the first to hear of Jesus' birth? Perhaps they were told because they represented the common people; they were not kings or military leaders. Perhaps they were told because Jesus himself would come to be understood as a shepherd, or because King David had been a shepherd. Or perhaps they were told just because the angels wanted to share the news with those close by.

492.

Shepherds were important in biblical times, and shepherd imagery is used throughout the Bible. In Luke 2:8–20, angels appear to shepherds tending their flocks at night to announce the birth of Jesus. These shepherds are honored to be some of the first to visit the Christ child. Later, in John 10:11, the adult Jesus tells his followers, "I am the good shepherd: the good shepherd giveth his life for the sheep."

493.

The most popular Christian holiday is Christmas, and yet the well-known and much-beloved Christmas stories of Jesus' birth are found in only two places in the Bible: Matthew 1 and 2, and Luke 1 and 2. Mark and John, both gospels about Jesus' life, don't even mention these wonderful stories.

494.

The Greek historian Herodotus (fifth century B.C.) spoke of magi who were a priestly tribe in the Persian empire. Later (in the book of Acts), the term refers to anyone who practiced magic arts (the word "magic" comes from *magi*). The most famous magi were the wise men who visited the baby Jesus.

495.

Only Matthew's gospel contains the account of the wise men bringing gifts of gold, frankincense, and myrrh. Luke's gospel relates other events surrounding Jesus' birth, but does not speak of the wise men.

496.

Tradition has it that three wise men came from the East (Persia, Babylonia, or Arabia) to visit the baby Jesus. Traditionally, their names were Melchior, Gaspar, and Balthasar. In fact, the Gospel of Matthew mentions neither their names nor how many they were. The number three arose from the gifts of gold, frankincense, and myrrh that they brought.

497.

Frankincense is a resin that was harvested from the tree of the same name; the resin was burned for its rich, pleasant smell. *Myrrh* came from Commiphora trees. Scripture records it as one of the gifts of the wise men at the birth of Jesus and as an embalming agent for him after the Crucifixion—so myrrh would seem special to Christians, as it was part of Christ's birth and death.

498.

Frankincense and myrrh were both expensive substances used to mask body odor, among other things. Baths and showers were not common, and frankincense was sometimes rubbed directly on the skin as a kind of deodorant. Women would stand over burning myrrh and allow the fragrance to permeate their clothes and hair before going out in public.

499.

The magi who came looking for Jesus probably came a year or more after Jesus was born. They were following a star, one which they likely believed was prophesied about 1,400 years earlier by Balaam: "There shall come a Star out of Jacob, and a Scepter shall rise out of Israel" (Numbers 24:17).

500.

The nature of the famous star that guided the wise men has remained elusive. Scientific suggestions have included a comet, a new star, a supernova, or a convergence of several planets. A comet was recorded about 4 B.C., and Jupiter, Mars, and Saturn converged in the constellation Pisces in 6 B.C. Both of these events could fit the biblical story.

501.

Micah predicted that Jesus would be born in Bethlehem about 700 years before it happened. So when the magi came to Jerusalem seeking an infant king, officials there could point them to Bethlehem, where King David had also been born. Mathew, Luke, and John all quote Micah. (See Micah 5:2.)

502.

According to the Gospel of Matthew, the wise men came looking for the child born "King of the Jews." When Herod heard this, he asked the wise men when the star appeared. Herod asked them to return word once they found the child so that he could worship him also. But the wise men were warned in a dream not to return to Herod, so they went home another way (Matthew 2:1–12).

503.

The Scripture does not say how many magi, or wise men, there were. It can be safely assumed the group was fairly large, both to travel safely some distance in the desert, and because their arrival in Jerusalem is said to have caused a great stir. Their particular office or title is not clear, but was of sufficient importance to give them immediate access to King Herod (Matthew 2:1–12).

504.

In the book of Matthew, Joseph was advised by an angel in a dream to flee the country and avoid King Herod, so he brought Mary and their infant Jesus to Egypt (Matthew 2:13).

505.

In describing the Slaughter of the Innocents by Herod, Matthew refers to "Rachel weeping for her children" (Matthew 2:18). Jacob's wife Rachel was buried near Bethlehem and venerated as the guardian of all mothers.

506.

Herod died when Jesus was still a young boy. He is buried at Herodium, but his tomb has never been discovered.

507.

Joseph returned with his family to Nazareth after Herod died. Herod's son, Herod Antipas, ruled Galilee at that time and rebuilt the city of Sepphoris. As a carpenter, Joseph would have easily found work there and provided for his family.

508.

At least seven provincial rulers or governors in the New Testament were named or called Herod. All of them were sons or relatives of Herod the Great through his several wives. His son Herod Antipas is the one who executed John the Baptist.

509.

When Mary and Joseph brought Jesus to Jerusalem for the purification ritual, they encountered a man named Simeon, who called Jesus, "A light to lighten the Gentiles, and the glory of thy people Israel" (Luke 2:32). Simeon was neither priest nor religious leader; he is only described as "a man in Jerusalem" who was "just and devout."

510.

The ancient city of Jerusalem has a history stretching back 6,000 years. By Jesus' time, the city had been fought over, conquered, destroyed, and rebuilt numerous times and had been under Roman rule since 63 B.C. It was one of the Holy Land's most cosmopolitan cities and a center of Roman administration.

511.

Jerusalem was divided into two parts, in addition to the massive temple complex. There was a Lower City where craftsmen and merchants worked and sold their wares, as well as an Upper City where the wealthy families lived. In the Upper City, a Roman market sold jewelry, fine leather, and other luxury goods.

512.

At the time of Christ, the population of Jerusalem was 35,000 to 40,000 people. During the holy days, such as Passover, the population may have swelled to several times that size, with perhaps as many as a quarter of a million Jews coming for Passover. The walled part of the city was only about one square mile.

513.

Anna praised God when Mary and Joseph brought the baby Jesus to the Temple. She is called a prophetess. Likely this did not refer to a profession but was a title of respect for a dignified and devout older woman.

514.

Jesus' family was not wealthy. When his parents brought him to the temple for the purification ceremony, they offered a sacrifice of two doves or pigeons, in obedience to the law. The normal sacrifice for this ceremony, however, was a lamb. Doves or pigeons were only to be offered by those who could not afford a lamb.

515.

In Jesus' day, the temple in Jerusalem reached up to 90 feet. No part of the temple exists today, except for an outer wall that surrounded the courtyard of the temple.

516.

The Romans did not destroy this section of the outer wall in part because it was not part of the temple itself. Today it is known most frequently as the "Western Wall" or the "Wailing Wall."

517.

The temple Jesus went to in Jerusalem was a renovation of the temple that the Jews built after the second exile. To enlarge the temple, King Herod had workers extend a platform over the south end of the temple hill. Only two stone blocks of the temple itself are known to remain.

518.

When Jesus was 12 years old, his family took him to the temple. At that age a young man became a "son of the commandment," personally responsible for knowing and keeping the Law. Even after his parents had started home, Jesus remained, listening to the elders teach and asking them questions. This, he said, was "My Father's business" (Luke 2:49).

519.

The Bible tells us about the birth of Jesus, and about a trip his family took to the temple when he was 12 years old. Other than that, we know little about his life until he began his ministry at the age of 30. We assume he was a carpenter because he was a carpenter's son. (See Mark 6:3 and Matthew 13:55.)

520.

Joseph is not called Jesus' father but "the husband of Mary, of whom Jesus was born." This was no doubt written to stress the importance of the virgin birth and the fact that Joseph was not Jesus' biological father.

521.

A Jewish boy was expected to learn and practice his father's trade. Each trade had its own symbol to wear, except on the Sabbath. A tailor had a needle in his tunic, and a carpenter, like Jesus and Joseph, wore a chip of wood behind his ear. The rabbis taught that a man who did not teach his son a trade brought him up to be a robber.

522.

The word translated from Hebrew as "carpenter" is *tekton*, a generic word for anyone who makes things. The word is applied to craftsmen of all sorts, but more frequently a builder. Early writings and tradition indicate Jesus worked with wood in some form—hence, carpenter.

523.

Carpenters and woodworkers made homes, tools for farming, and weapons for war. Some artisans became metal workers, shaping tools, weapons, and jewelry.

524.

The gospels are firmly rooted in historical fact. Luke, for example, names the specific year, emperor, governor, tetrarchs, and high priests in office when John the Baptist began to preach near the Jordan River (Luke 3:1–2).

525.

Luke was the only gentile among the New Testament's authors, and he wrote for a gentile audience. As a medical doctor, he tells us that he investigated his subject matter thoroughly before setting forth his account (Luke 1:1–4), and his eye for details is evident. His book also has a warm, human touch to it.

526.

Mark 1:9 describes Jesus' baptism by John in the Jordan River. The Jordan River runs south from the Sea of Galilee into the Dead Sea, a landlocked salt lake.

527.

The Jordan River, where Jesus was baptized, had little economic or political significance. It was too small for transporting goods and easily forded during the dry summer months. Its significance is mostly historical and spiritual (Deuteronomy 9, 11).

528.

The name of the Jordan River comes from a word that means "descender." The river itself drops over 2,000 feet from its source near Mt. Hebron to the Dead Sea, which is below sea level. Although the distance between these two points is a little less than 100 miles, the river winds and bends so much that its actual length is almost twice that.

529.

The Dead Sea, as its name implies, contains almost no life forms because its salinity (saltiness) is too high. The landlocked Dead Sea lies in a desert. When its waters evaporate in the heat, salty minerals are left behind, causing the remaining water to become saltier.

530.

John the Baptist, who pointed the way to Jesus and baptized him, lived an ascetic life in the Judean wilderness near the Dead Sea. He survived on simple desert fare, eating whatever the desert provided. His dress was also rustic: He wore a tunic of camel's hair with a leather belt.

531.

Garments made from the hair of goats, sheep, and camels are often called "sackcloth," which was the clothing of the poor, the powerless, and the mourning. In Matthew 3:4–5, John the Baptist wears a camel hair shirt to show his humility and devoutness as he prepares the way for Jesus.

532.

John the Baptist was said to eat "locusts and wild honey" (Matthew 3:4 and Mark 1:6).

533.

The Roman historian Josephus has more to say about John the Baptist than about Jesus. John was so famous, in fact, that the word Baptist was coined to describe him—it did not exist as a noun before that. It was John, however, who said that, "[Jesus] must increase, but I must decrease" (John 3:30).

534.

We only know fragments of the relationship between Jesus and John the Baptist. Their mothers were cousins, but they grew up in separate towns, with a four-day walk between them. The gospels give us only a few direct interactions between the men, but they were obviously aware of each other. At one point, Jesus declared of John, "Verily I say unto you, Among them that are born of women there hath not risen a greater than John the Baptist" (Matthew 11:11).

535.

John the Baptist protested when Jesus wanted to be baptized, because he knew Jesus did not have to repent of any sins. But Jesus insisted, because he wanted to identify with his cousin John and the people he was baptizing. He was saying he wanted to live a righteous life under God's rules.

536.

Jesus' ministry did not begin in the temple or synagogue or within the capital city of his day. Instead, it began at his baptism. What may stand out the most about Jesus' baptism is not who was involved or where it was done. What stands out the most is a clear sense of call and appointment of Jesus of Nazareth.

537.

Jesus was baptized near Jericho in the lower Jordan. The site is also near Mt. Nebo, where Moses saw the Promised Land, and near Bethel, where Abraham built an altar. Nearby, Jacob saw a ladder ascending into heaven, and Elijah was taken up in a chariot and fed by ravens.

538.

At Passover, a lamb was slaughtered and its blood splashed on the lintels of the door, at the top and on the sides. Christians believe this resembles a person splayed out on a cross. John the Baptist called Jesus the "Lamb of God" (John 1:29).

539.

Although the gospel of John speaks about John the Baptist's ministry and John the Baptist testifying to Jesus being the Lamb of God, the gospel does not show an actual baptism.

540.

Winnowing involved separating the wheat from its husk by beating the grain and then tossing the mixture into the air. The heavier grain would fall to the ground, while the wind would blow the rest away. John the Baptist used this process to describe how Christ would separate believers from unbelievers (Matthew 3:12).

541.

John the Baptist introduced some of his disciples to Jesus, and they spent several days with him. After they returned home, Jesus went back and called them again as apostles. These men included two sets of brothers: Simon Peter and Andrew, as well as James and John. (See Matthew 4:18–22.)

542.

The disciples were not all poor peasants. Peter, James, John, and Andrew were partners in a successful fishing business. They owned homes and had servants. Fish from the Sea of Galilee was preserved and sold as far away as Spain. Matthew, the tax collector, also had a large home.

543.

Peter was a successful fisherman, with a home in Capernaum and a wife who traveled with him in his work as an apostle. He was energetic, enthusiastic, and impulsive. Peter's given name was Simon, but Jesus changed his name to Peter when they met while John was baptizing in the Jordan River.

544.

Jesus met his disciples James and John while they were mending nets in a ship on the Sea of Galilee (Matthew 4:21).

545.

Zebedee was the father of apostles James and John. When called, both James and John left the ship and their father to follow Jesus (Matthew 4:21–22 and Mark 1:19–20).

546.

The Apostle John, son of Zebedee and Salome, was well connected. Besides their fishing business in Galilee, his family owned a home in Jerusalem (John 19:27) and were friends with the high priest (John 18:15–16).

547.

The Apostle John may have been a childhood friend of Jesus, since their mothers appear to be related. He followed Jesus from the beginning of his ministry, and calls himself "the disciple whom Jesus loved." After writing five New Testament books, he was exiled to an island for several years and died of natural causes in Ephesus around A.D. 100.

548.

The New Testament mentions several different types of nets used in fishing. These include the small cast net that was thrown out into the water by hand, and the large drag net that was several hundred yards long and whose two ends were laboriously hauled into shore. Many of Jesus' disciples were fishermen, and the Bible also mentions the work of maintaining the nets, including washing (Luke 5:2), spreading and drying (Ezekiel 47:10), and mending (Matthew 4:21).

549.

In Jeremiah 16:16–21 the Lord says, "I will send for many fishers" and they will fish for evildoers, so "I will cause them to know mine hand and my might; and they shall know that my name is The Lord." Jesus chose at least four fishermen among his disciples.

550.

Students usually chose which rabbi they wanted to follow and learn from, but Jesus chose his disciples. Sometimes he taught only them, and sometimes he elaborated to them after teaching others. It was common for a rabbi to be followed by a group of disciples.

551.

A rabbi was someone respected for their knowledge and understanding. The word comes from a Hebrew word that means "Great One" and had come to mean "teacher" or "master." Jesus never objected to being called rabbi or master, although he cautioned the elders and his disciples not to seek such titles, because "whosoever shall exalt himself shall be abased" (Matthew 23:12).

552.

We tend to think of only twelve disciples, but Jesus had more followers than that. At one time he sent out 70 others to preach (Luke 10:1). After the resurrection he appeared to at least 500 of them at one time (see 1 Corinthians 15:6). The Twelve were especially close to him, and were later called apostles.

553.

The disciples most likely joined Jesus believing they would become leaders in some new political order. Even John the Baptist saw Jesus in this way (Matthew 11:3). In fact, the last question the disciples asked, even after the resurrection, was, "Lord, wilt thou at this time restore again the kingdom to Israel?" (Acts 1:6).

554.

Jesus took over a year to choose his disciples. While John, Andrew, Peter, Philip and Nathaniel began to follow him about the time of his baptism in late A.D. 26, he didn't call Simon, Andrew, James, and John to actually leave their fishing business until almost a year later, and he called Matthew after that. The formal call of the twelve was not until as late as May of A.D. 28.

555.

The number 12 has significance in the Bible. It refers to the 12 tribes of Israel, and also to the 12 apostles: Simon Peter, Andrew, James and his brother John, Philip, Bartholomew, Thomas, Matthew, James, Thaddaeus, Simon, and Judas Iscariot.

556.

The apostles were a close-knit group, with two or three sets of brothers and possibly one father and son. There were also two called James, two called Simon, and two called Judas. Some of them were referred to with nicknames—"the Zealot," "the Twin," and the "Sons of Thunder."

557.

One of Jesus' disciples, Simon the Zealot, was a terrorist—at least to the Romans. The Zealots were bent on driving the Romans out of Palestine. Simon is only mentioned three times. Since Jesus also selected Matthew—who was a tax collector for the Romans—as a disciple, he was clearly reaching out to everyone.

558.

Matthew was a former tax collector who became one of the 12 apostles. He wrote one of the four gospels, detailing Jesus' earthly ministry, which became the first book of the New Testament. Mark and Luke both include the story of Matthew's calling, but they refer to him as Levi. This was probably a family surname.

559.

The book of Matthew does not name its author, but John's pupil Papias says Matthew wrote it. The early church universally accepted this view. Matthew describes himself in the book only as a publican (tax collector).

560.

The four Gospels give us an account of Christ's life. Matthew, Mark, and Luke are more chronological, yet they start at different points and include different details. John's Gospel is an essay that makes certain points to prove that Jesus was the Son of God.

561.

Salt was used to seal covenants because its preservative qualities made it a fitting symbol for long-lasting agreements. When Jesus said his followers should be "the salt of the earth" (Matthew 5:13), he was suggesting something about the quality of our relationships with each other.

562.

After he was baptized by John the Baptist, Jesus went into an extremely rugged wilderness near the Jordan River. There, after going without food for 40 days, he was tempted by Satan. Throughout the Gospels Jesus often walked great distances or stayed up all night to pray.

563.

The word "devil" comes from Greek *diablos* ("slanderer"), while "Satan" comes from Hebrew *satan* ("adversary"). The New Testament gives us most of our information about the devil, showing him as a malevolent reality, always opposed to God and his people, and whose power will be crushed in the end. He appears in many forms, such as a serpent, a dragon, a sea monster, a flash of lightning, an angel of light, and a roaring lion.

564.

Jesus' fasting and temptation mainly occurred in the Judean Desert. Satan was in charge of the 40 days of temptation, which began when he tempted Jesus to break his fast by turning rocks into bread. Satan then tried to provoke Jesus to jump from a pinnacle and wait for angels to catch him. Finally, he took Jesus to a mountaintop and tempted him with the kingship of the world.

565.

Jesus fasted for 40 days to prepare for the Temptation in the mountains, Moses fasted for 40 days to prepare to receive the Ten Commandments on Mt. Sinai, and Elijah fasted for 40 days on his way to Mt. Horeb. These three appeared together on the Mount of Transfiguration.

566.

In the Bible, the number 40 represents the development and history of salvation: testing. Jesus fasted in the wilderness for "forty days and forty nights" (Matthew 4:2), and the Bible text plainly records "he was afterward an hungred"—which is hardly surprising.

567.

The book of Hebrews states that Jesus, even though he was God, was tempted to sin just as we are, but he was able to resist the temptation (4:15). This is part of an argument that he identifies with our struggles. The Bible says nothing about the normal temptations he probably faced growing up.

568.

Mark was the first written Gospel (around A.D. 50), followed by several of Paul's letters to the churches. Luke completed his Gospel and the book of Acts before Paul died in A.D. 65. The other Gospels and letters from Peter and Jude followed. The last books written were John's three letters, his Gospel, and the Book of the Revelation, all after A.D. 90.

569.

Mark's account of Jesus' life is the shortest and the most action-oriented. Mark portrays Jesus as one who was constantly serving others. Mark records 18 miracles and only 4 full parables. In contrast, a much greater emphasis on Jesus' teachings is in the other gospels.

570.

The Apostle John's picture of Jesus is the most theological of the four Gospels. His focus is upon Jesus as the Son of God the Father. His book is addressed to the world at large, and his purpose was to convince people that Jesus was the Messiah, the Son of God (John 20:31). The action is slower than in Mark's Gospel, with more attention to conversations and teaching.

571.

The Apostle John was probably the author of the book of John, but he is not mentioned by name in the book. Instead, he refers to himself as "the disciple whom Jesus loved" or by some other means. For example, he says this about his own witnessing of Jesus' death: "And he that saw it bare record, and his record is true: and he knoweth that he saith true, that ye might believe" (John 19:35).

572.

In the first chapter of his Gospel, the Apostle John argues that the Word has a name—Jesus. The Word, he says, "was made flesh, and dwelt among us, (and we beheld his glory…)" (John 1:14). The Greeks, the Romans, the Egyptians, the Assyrians, the Jews—everyone at that time used the idea of the Word to describe God's character or personality.

573.

There are seven titles for Jesus in the first chapter of John alone. In this one passage of scripture, he is called the Word of God, the Lamb of God, the Son of God, Rabbi, Messiah, the King of Israel, and the Son of Man.

574.

Jesus referred to himself as the "Son of Man," a somewhat ambiguous term with several possible meanings at that time. It emphasized his humanity, but most Jews would have remembered that the prophet Daniel described the coming Messiah as "one like the Son of man" (Daniel 7:13).

575.

In the Gospel of John, Jesus is referred to as "the lamb of God, which taketh away the sin of the world." The exact meaning of this phrase has caused much debate among biblical scholars. Some believe John saw Jesus as a symbolic sacrificial lamb for the atonement of all sins, while others believe he may have been referring to the horned ram that led a flock, the traditional symbol of the king of Israel.

576.

The first few sentences of the Gospel of John were from a song that the early church sang about the deity of Christ. The Apostle John spent three years with Jesus, but by the time he wrote his gospel, he had 50 years to reflect on his experience. His account is different from the other three Gospels, but not contradictory.

577.

During biblical times, people were much less precise about time. Most did not observe their birthdays or even know their own exact ages. Those who kept track used landmark events like floods or the reign of a king. Luke tells us Jesus was "about thirty" when he began his ministry (Luke 3:23).

578.

Jesus spent almost all of the first year and a half of his public ministry in the region of Galilee, where he grew up. Many important highways passed through Galilee, going to distant places. Thus, Jesus could have had easy contact with a wide variety of people without traveling very far and without exposing himself early in his ministry to the anger of the religious authorities in Jerusalem.

579.

Matthew covers the first year of Christ's ministry in Galilee in two verses, Matthew 4:11–12, although the events during this period were also covered by John (1:19–4:54) and Luke (4:16–30). Matthew devotes almost half of his book to the rest of the time Jesus spent in Galilee, however, while John hardly mentions this time.

580.

The temple that Jesus knew was first built in 516 B.C. It lacked the magnificence of Solomon's Temple, but it was functional. Predicting his own resurrection, Jesus once said he could rebuild the "temple" in three days. His opponents commented, "Forty and six years was this temple in building, and wilt thou rear it up in three days?" (John 2:20).

581.

The temple was greatly expanded by King Herod and his successors into a structure with many impressive courtyards, chambers, colonnades, and gates around it. Jesus had foreseen that it would be destroyed.

582.

The temple itself was built in only 18 months, and priests were trained to do the work since laymen were not allowed to touch it. All the details of the outer courts took 80 years to complete, long after Herod himself had died. The temple complex was completed around A.D. 64, just a few years before the entire thing was razed by the Romans.

583.

Herod's temple was twice the size of the second temple, with an outer Court of the Gentiles that was about 1,000 feet wide by 1,500 feet long. Inside that perimeter was a courtyard where only Jews, including women, were allowed, and inside *that* was a courtyard for Jewish men only. Then, surrounding the sanctuary, was a courtyard for only priests.

584.

The book of 3 John is the shortest book in the Bible, with 4 fewer words than its companion book, 2 John. Both of these were about one papyrus sheet in length. Five books share the distinction of being only one chapter long: Obadiah (in the Old Testament) and Philemon, 2 John, 3 John, and Jude (in the New Testament).

585.

There were essentially three political parties at the time of Christ. The Pharisees were very strict about the Law and were anti-Roman. The Sadducees were more liberal, and hoped to accommodate Rome in some ways. Finally, the Herodians had little theological interest and collaborated with King Herod. All three groups were ultimately allied in putting Jesus to death.

586.

The Zealots were a splinter group of the Pharisees who wanted to drive out the Romans. The movement was centered in Galilee, where Jesus spent most of his ministry. This may explain why one of his disciples had been a Zealot. The Zealots began an uprising a few years after his death, which ended in A.D. 70 with the destruction of the temple.

587.

The Pharisees were a political and religious party that began about 200 years before the life of Christ. The name comes from a word that means "separate," and their original concern was defending Jewish tradition from the influence of Greek culture. They became experts in Old Testament law. There were about 6,000 of them when Jesus was alive.

588.

Jesus had many run-ins with Pharisees, especially about the hypocrisy of some. Because of this, "pharisaical" has come to mean hypocritical or sanctimonious. However, the original impulse of the Pharisees was noble: To follow and obey God's Law in every area of life.

589.

The Pharisees believed that when the Messiah came he would judge gentiles and other sinners, but from the beginning Jesus was more concerned about money changers in the temple and other disturbing aspects of religious tradition.

590.

Nicodemus was a devout Pharisee leader who came to Jesus by night to inquire about Jesus' teachings (John 3). Jesus had an extended discussion with him, telling the Pharisee leader that he did not come to punish sinners but to rescue them, and it appears that Nicodemus became a follower of Jesus while still remaining a Pharisee. Later, Nicodemus defended Jesus in the Sanhedrin, at some risk to his own reputation (John 7:50–52), and he helped to bury Jesus' body (John 19:39–42).

591.

Jesus was the first one to use the term "born again," in conversation with Nicodemus. Nicodemus was confused by this, but Jesus explained that he was talking about a spiritual birth, not a physical one. Without this, Jesus said, one "cannot see the kingdom of God" (John 3:3).

592.

When Jesus explained being born again to Nicodemus, three times he said "verily" or "most assuredly." The word is literally "amen" in Hebrew. Nicodemus would have understood this as meaning Jesus was absolutely certain, and the idea was binding and necessary.

593.

The disciples were surprised to find Jesus talking to the woman at the well, not just because she was a woman but also because she was a Samaritan. (See John 4.) The Samaritans did not recognize any prophets after Moses and only accepted the first five books of the Old Testament.

594.

When Jesus and his disciples walked from Galilee to Jerusalem for the holy days, like most pilgrims they usually did not take a direct route. They traveled east first, and then south along the Jordan River valley, avoiding the more mountainous Samaria, as well as the Samaritans themselves. The trek was about 90 miles and would have taken three or four days.

595.

The Samaritans were despised because they were viewed as a mixed race that practiced a corrupt form of Jewish worship at Mount Gerizim rather than at Jerusalem. The woman Jesus encountered at the well in John 4 was a Samaritan. Jesus also told a well-known story about the Good Samaritan.

596.

The synagogue became the center of Jewish community life when the Jews were exiled to Babylon (597 B.C.) and the temple was destroyed. Even though Herod had rebuilt the temple by the time of Jesus, the synagogue still functioned in each town as a school, social center, and meeting place.

597.

Jesus attended synagogue each Sabbath and often preached there. The custom was for seven men to mount the platform called a bima and read from the scriptures. According to custom, the reader would read in Hebrew while an interpreter would translate it into Aramaic, the everyday language. Then the man would sit down and explain what he had read.

598.

Although in Jesus' day only a few people could read—and fewer still could write—it is clear Jesus could do both. We see him reading in the synagogue and writing in the dirt. The synagogue was the central institution for Jews outside the temple, and some ability to read Hebrew was expected of most men.

599.

Jesus was multilingual. Most everyday conversation in Palestine was in Aramaic, but Jesus also knew Hebrew. The trade language of the day was Greek, spoken to foreigners (including the Romans) since the time of Alexander the Great.

600.

Many Hebrew or Aramaic words are used in modern-day worship. *Hallelujah* means "Praise the Lord!" *Hosanna* was a shout of acclamation used to welcome Jesus into Jerusalem, which originally meant "Save us!" *Amen* is Hebrew for "Surely! So be it!" *Maranatha* was an Aramaic word used by Paul meaning "Our Lord, come!" (referring to hopes of Christ's return to earth).

601.

Aramaic, which is closely related to Hebrew, all but died out in the centuries following Jesus' day. Amazingly, the language still survives today, but only in isolated villages in Syria, Turkey, Iraq, and Iran. Assyrian Christians from northern Iraq still speak it today as well.

602.

Luke 4:16–21 is sometimes called the Jesus Manifesto. This is where Jesus read from Isaiah in the synagogue at Nazareth and said the prophecy was fulfilled that day. The components of this manifesto were preaching the good news, freeing captives, and giving sight to the blind. He also proclaimed the "year of the Lord," a reference to the year of Jubilee when all debts were forgiven.

603.

Christians believe that the promises made in the book of Isaiah were fulfilled in the Gospels. Because of this, Isaiah is often called the fifth Gospel. The New Testament itself is a champion of Isaiah's, citing him 419 times!

604.

One Sabbath at the synagogue in his hometown of Nazareth, Jesus read from the scriptures about the Messiah coming. Then he said the passage referred to him, but that he was not going to heal anyone there. The people of Nazareth were so angry that they tried to throw him off a cliff. (See Luke 4:16–30.)

605.

"Physician, heal thyself" was a skeptical challenge that Jesus predicted the people from his hometown would hurl at him when he tried to do miracles there. It could be paraphrased as follows: You heal others so well, let's see you heal yourself. Jesus called it a proverb, indicating that it must have been a common phrase. The attitude it expresses is "you have done so well elsewhere, let's see you do the same here."

606.

Nazareth, the childhood home of Jesus, was a very small farming town high in a sheltered valley, some 1,300 feet above sea level. The first-century Jewish historian Josephus said the area was so fertile that "even the most indolent. . . are tempted to devote themselves to agriculture." Jesus is thought to have drawn many of his rural illustrations from his childhood in this farming community.

607.

Nazareth has only one spring, and it never runs dry. The water flows into a well where women still gather and fill jugs that they balance on their heads, much like Mary would have done.

608.

Elijah once found refuge in the home of a pagan widow, and Elisha healed a pagan general named Naaman of leprosy. Jesus pointed to these two examples when he told people from his hometown of Nazareth that "no prophet is accepted in his own country" (Luke 4:24). Over and over again, he asserted that the gospel message was not just for the Jews.

609.

When Jesus cast out a demon (Luke 4:35–36), the people said he had power and authority. The Greek word translated as "authority" means freedom of choice and action. What they meant was that Jesus acted spontaneously, on his own, without permission.

610.

Humans did not always obey Jesus—he told them not to discuss what he had done but they did anyway (Mark 1:43–45). But the demons always obeyed him, frequently acknowledged they knew who he was, and were in awe of him (Mark 1:24).

611.

The word translated as "bushel" refers to a measure of around three gallons of grain. In any household there was a container of this size to measure the wheat or barley needed for making bread. Poorer households also used this container as a table. "Neither do men light a candle, and put it under a bushel, but on a candlestick," Jesus said (Matthew 5:15).

612.

Ordinary people lived in small, one- or two-room houses. The roofs were flat (because it seldom rained) and used as patios for people to get fresh air without standing in the street. Jesus said you could put a lamp on a stand and "it giveth light unto all that are in the house" (Matthew 5:15), a reference to these small homes.

613.

When Jesus said, "one jot or one tittle shall in no wise pass from the law, till all be fulfilled" (Matthew 5:18), he affirmed the importance of the Old Testament law. The "jot" was the *yodh*, the smallest letter of the Hebrew alphabet, while the "tittle" was only part of a letter: a small pen stroke.

614.

Jesus spoke about empty-headed people when he said, "And whosoever shall say to his brother, Raca, shall be in danger of the council" (Matthew 5:22). The Aramaic word is one of insult, related to the Hebrew term for empty. It means something like empty-headed one (airhead or blockhead).

615.

Judges were powerful men given their responsibilities as an honor. They were not paid but were respected and even feared. Any Israelite could be a civil judge, but only a priest could decide a criminal case. Their power was so great that Jesus advised making peace with your opponent before you even got to court, "lest at any time the adversary deliver thee to the judge" (Matthew 5:25).

616.

Under Roman occupation, any crime the Romans considered too petty to bother with would be handed over to the local Jewish authorities. Such was the case in John 8:3–7, when the Pharisees brought an adulterous woman to Jesus and asked him what her punishment should be. Jesus replied, "He that is without sin among you, let him first cast a stone at her."

617.

The first 11 verses of John 8, which tell the story of the woman accused of adultery, do not appear in the earliest and oldest New Testament manuscripts. These verses may have been added later by someone with knowledge of the event, and the passage certainly seems consistent with the way Jesus taught and acted.

618.

Matthew gathered the teachings of Jesus into five sections, the longest and best-known of which is the Sermon on the Mount (Matthew 5–7). The sections of teachings are alternated with narratives about what Jesus did and where he went.

619.

Jesus gave six lengthy discourses in scripture, plus many other teachings. Any of them can be read in a short amount of time. The most famous of these is the Sermon on the Mount (see Matthew 5). Each Gospel writer tended to share different points from what was probably a longer speech, so seeing the big picture usually requires comparing the different accounts.

620.

When Jesus refers to the Scriptures, he is referring to the Old Testament. The Scriptures at that time had the same material as the Old Testament today but in a different order. It is thought that the prophet Ezra collected and restored these writings as the Jews returned from captivity in Babylon and rebuilt the temple.

621.

Some scholars believe Jesus gave his Sermon on the Mount atop a hill on the north end of the Sea of Galilee that acts as a natural amphitheater. Voices are naturally amplified there, so Jesus, speaking in a normal voice, could easily have been heard as far as 200 yards away.

622.

The Sea of Galilee is the world's lowest freshwater lake, at 680 feet below sea level. It is about 13 miles long and 8 miles wide, with rugged hills rising abruptly from its eastern and western shores. Its position below sea level and flank of high mountains on the east make it susceptible to severe weather changes and great storms, some of which we read about in the New Testament.

623.

Several of the disciples were fishermen on the Sea of Galilee, home to over 40 species of fish, which were dried or salted and exported throughout the region.

624.

The Sea of Galilee was also known as the Lake of Chinnereth, the Sea of Tiberias, and the Lake of Gennesaret (John 6:1).

625.

When Jesus referred to a "city on a hill" in the Sermon on the Mount, he may have been thinking of his own hometown of Nazareth. Nazareth was on a hill and its light could be seen from Cana, nine miles away.

626.

When Jesus tells his disciples not to worry, because his Father takes care of and feeds even the birds, he refers specifically to ravens (Luke 12:24). Ravens were considered unclean, and his listeners would not have seen this example as poetic but as disgusting. It would be like saying that God loved vultures, not just songbirds.

627.

Jesus used animal references in his teachings. During his Sermon on the Mount, he observes, "Behold the fowls of the air: for they sow not, neither do they reap, nor gather into barns; yet your heavenly Father feedeth them. Are ye not much better than they?" Other animals used in his teachings include dogs and swine.

628.

The expression "Let your yes be yes" comes from Jesus' words in the Sermon on the Mount, when he stated that people should not swear falsely, nor should they take any oaths by heaven or by Jerusalem or by anything else. A simple yes or no should be binding: "Let your communication be, Yea, yea; Nay, nay" (Matthew 5:37).

629.

In Jesus' Sermon on the Mount, he spoke in detail about ethical living. He said, for example, "But whoever shall smite thee on thy right cheek, turn to him the other also" (Matthew 5:39). This made the point about not seeking revenge for injury, but forgiving wrongdoers.

630.

The idea expressed in Matthew 5:39 is also found in Lamentations 3:30, advising, "He giveth his cheek to him that smiteth him." Jesus often expanded on Old Testament teaching in this way.

631.

In the Sermon on the Mount, Jesus spoke repeatedly about going beyond the minimal requirements of law or social courtesy in order to show true generosity of spirit. One vivid illustration was when he said, "And whosoever shall compel thee to go a mile, go with him twain" (Matthew 5:41). This referred to a detested Roman practice of forcing civilians into the service of carrying military baggage for a prescribed distance, one Roman mile.

632.

In the Sermon on the Mount, Jesus said, "Give not that which is holy unto the dogs, neither cast ye your pearls before swine, lest they trample them under their feet, and turn again and rend you." Holy things and pearls here represent the truths of the Gospel, and dogs and pigs represent any people who have become cynical and hardened against God's word. The saying emphasized the importance of choosing how and where to preach the Gospel.

633.

In Luke's account of the Sermon on the Mount, Jesus "came down with them, and stood in the plain" (Luke 6:17). In Matthew's account, he "went up into a mountain, and sat down there" (Matthew 15:29). It is possible he did both things in the same sermon, but more likely he gave the same sermon more than once. He was teaching continually and may have discussed the same ideas hundreds of times.

634.

While prayer was to be practiced at any time, even unceasingly, it was to be done meaningfully. Jesus warned about idly and endlessly repeating empty phrases in prayer (Matthew 6:7).

635.

Rich people's homes were stone, but everyone else's homes were made of handmade bricks of clay and straw. These were burgled easily and often, and Jesus referred to this when he said to lay up treasure in heaven where "thieves do not break through nor steal" (Matthew 6:20).

636.

Rich people had chairs and tables, but most people sat or slept on the ground, even in their homes. Most homes had chests for storing food and clothes. These chests doubled as tables. Homes like those in Capernaum (where Jesus stayed with his disciples) did have rooms, because they often housed two or more families.

637.

The word *mammon* comes from an Aramaic term (*mamona*) meaning "wealth." Jesus gave negative connotations to the term when he said, "Ye cannot serve God and mammon" (Matthew 6:24) and when he referred to "unrighteous mammon" (Luke 16:11). The latter term probably referred to ill-gotten gains.

638.

Jesus compared the kingdom of heaven to a pearl, saying, "The kingdom of heaven is like unto a merchant man, seeking goodly pearls: Who, when he had found one pearl of great price, went and sold all that he had, and bought it" (Matthew 13:45–46).

639.

In Matthew 7:1, Jesus says, "Judge not, that ye be not judged." This text is not meant to be a diatribe against all discernment. It's a warning against hypocrisy, criticizing others for the things we're doing.

640.

The word "Shiloh" was used in Genesis 49:10 as an early reference to the Messiah: "The scepter shall not depart from Judah, nor a lawgiver from between his feet, until Shiloh come." The word means "to rest" or "to give rest." Jesus said to come to him and he would "give you rest" (Matthew 11:28).

641.

Jesus used hyperbole and figurative language very effectively when he scolded people for noticing motes in other people's eyes while ignoring the beams in their own eyes (Matthew 7:3–5).

642.

Simon Peter fell to Jesus' knees and said, "Depart from me; for I am a sinful man, O Lord." Simon Peter said this after seeing Jesus perform a miracle with a draught of fish (Luke 5:3–9).

643.

There are 35 recorded miracles, 17 of which include healing. But seven specific passages refer to Christ healing many more people than this. For example, multitudes came to him and he "healed them all" (Luke 6:17–19).

644.

The account of Jesus healing Simon Peter's mother-in-law is found in all gospels except the gospel of John. See Matthew 8:14–15, Mark 1:29–31, and Luke 4:38–39.

645.

Jesus performed many miracles, including restoring sight to the blind, feeding thousands with a handful of food, and walking on water. But perhaps his most astounding miracle was the resurrection of the dead.

646.

Jesus raised three people from the dead. He raised the son of a widow from Nain when he encountered his funeral procession. Then he raised the 12-year-old daughter of Jairus. And finally he raised his friend Lazarus, the brother of Mary and Martha (Luke 7:11–15, 8:41–56, Matthew 9:18–25, Mark 5:21–42, and John 11:1–44).

647.

Jesus raised the adult son of the widow from Nain from the dead during a funeral procession. "He had compassion on her," Luke writes (Luke 7:13). She had lost her husband and her only son, and there was no one to take care of her.

648.

In a funeral procession, male relatives carried the body on a bier, while the women walked ahead. Signs of mourning included wailing and tearing of clothes. Professional mourners and flute players were hired to show how much sorrow (or status) the family had. Jesus encountered such processions several times.

649.

A synagogue leader begged Jesus to come to his 12-year-old daughter's deathbed and heal her. By the time Jesus arrived, mourners had assembled, bewailing the girl's death. But Jesus announced that the girl was only sleeping. Some scoffed, but Jesus took her by the hand and said, "Talitha cumi; which is, being interpreted, Damsel, I say unto thee, arise" (Mark 5:41). Immediately she got up and walked around.

650.

While the gospels of Matthew, Mark, and Luke all contain the story of Jesus raising the daughter of a synagogue ruler from the dead, only Mark and Luke give the name of the ruler, Jairus (Matthew 9:18–26, Mark 5:21–43, and Luke 8:40–56).

651.

Jairus's daughter, who was raised from the dead, wasn't named. Jairus, the synagogue leader, didn't refer to her by name. When raising her, Jesus called her a "damsel" in the Gospel of Mark and a "maid" in Matthew and Luke (Matthew 9:18, 23–26, Mark 5:22–23, 35–42, and Luke 8:41–42, 49–55).

652.

Most of Jesus' miracles took place in a small area on the north side of the Sea of Galilee. This included Capernaum, Chorazin, and Bethsaida. The miracles provoked so little response that Jesus said several notably wicked cities in the Old Testament (including Sodom) would have repented if they had seen what he was doing (Matthew 11:20–24).

653.

Fishing was an important and respected occupation near the Sea of Galilee, as evidenced by the names of towns where Jesus lived and ministered: Bethsaida means "the fishery" and Magdala means "fish tower."

654.

Since his steps took him across the Galilee countryside quite often, Jesus did much of his teaching on the way from one town of Galilee to another: Cana, Tiberias, Nazareth, and Capernaum. All his walks along the western shore of the Sea of Galilee passed through the Galilean fishing villages where he performed some of his best-known miracles.

655.

Jesus spent so much time in Capernaum that it was considered his hometown (Matthew 9:1). There were about 1,500 people at that time, including a Roman garrison under the control of Herod Antipas. The commanding centurion was friendly and supportive of his Jewish neighbors and built the synagogue for them. Jesus healed the centurion's servant (Luke 7:1–9).

656.

The account of Jesus healing the servant of the Centurion is found in every gospel except the gospel of Mark. As related in Matthew 8:5–13, when Jesus approaches Capernaum, a centurion comes to him to ask for help, but says that Jesus does not have to go to the servant, saying, "I am not worthy that thou shouldest come under my roof: but speak the word only, and my servant shall be healed." A very similar account is found in Luke 7:1–10, although in Luke's account the centurion sends his request for help through intermediaries. John 4:46–54 relays an account of a nobleman at Capernaum who requests help from Jesus for his sick son, whom Jesus heals from afar.

657.

In Capernaum, so many people mobbed a house where Jesus was teaching that the door was blocked. When four men arrived with a paralyzed man on a stretcher, they couldn't get in. So they improvised: They took the man up to the roof, cut a hole through the plaster, and lowered the stretcher down to Jesus. Jesus was so moved by this display of faith that he immediately healed the man.

658.

Several times when Jesus healed someone, he told that person not to tell anyone about it. For example, he gave this command to a couple of blind men after healing them, but they told others anyway (Matthew 9:27–31). Scholars say that either Jesus did not want the miracles to distract from what he was trying to teach, or he wanted to wait for the right moment to reveal who he was.

659.

Jesus said several times not to tell anyone about him or about his miracles (Mark 8:30). He did not want anyone to misunderstand him or force his hand, because a group of militants called Zealots wanted the Messiah to set up a political kingdom in northern Galilee.

660.

Suspected lepers were quarantined for seven days and then examined by a priest. If the condition persisted, they were quarantined for another seven days and examined again. At this point, they were forbidden to have any contact with healthy humans, including their own families, and became outcasts and beggars. Jesus healed and befriended many of them.

661.

One leper felt something he had probably not felt in a very long time when Jesus "put forth his hand, and touched him" (Matthew 8:3). Many people at that time believed leprosy was a result of one's sin, and so the psychological impact of the disease was often as bad as the disease itself. The first-century Jewish historian Josephus tells us that these "untouchables" could live for ten or more years with the disease, and were treated as dead men.

662.

Jesus angered the Pharisees when he healed a man with a withered hand (Matthew 12:10–14, Mark 3:1–6, Luke 6:6–11).

663.

Jesus healed a crippled woman on the Sabbath, and the Jewish leaders were enraged. Even though she had been unable to stand up straight for 18 years, the leader of the synagogue told her she should have come back on a different day to be healed (Luke 13:10–17).

664.

Sabbath began each week when the first three stars appeared on Friday evening. A trumpet was blown, calling people from their work to supper. They did not eat again until after the service in the synagogue the next day. No household work could be done on the Sabbath, so meals were prepared ahead of time. Jesus was once criticized for snacking on grain on the Sabbath (Mark 2:23–27).

665.

Daily life in the city began at sunrise, and most official business was concluded before noon. Life was structured to slow down in the heat of the day, and dinner started as early as 3:30, as it was not safe to be out after dark. Most of the dinners Jesus attended were in daylight.

666.

Jesus frequently attended feasts, which often went on for five or six hours, accompanied by music and dancing, and was even criticized by his enemies for attending such events with nonreligious Jews and even gentiles. (See Mark 2:13–17.)

667.

Wealthy men often invited friends, clients, and social climbers to dinner with written invitations delivered and read by servants. Other guests were invited on impulse during the day. They invited people who could do them favors or who were celebrities, which explains why Jesus was often invited to lavish dinners.

668.

We are never told that Jesus laughed, but children were attracted to him, and he was often welcome at parties with tax collectors and prostitutes. This suggests a welcoming demeanor toward those who are often overlooked or mistreated. And his Father laughs—see Psalm 59:8—so it's likely he did, too!

669.

At one dinner party Jesus is described as sitting at the table while a woman standing behind him washed his feet (Luke 7:36–50). This sounds awkward, but Jesus would have been reclining with his feet away from the table. The woman could have slipped into the dinner unnoticed because it was customary for servants to stand by their masters' feet during a meal.

670.

Since people wore sandals in dusty Bible lands, their feet had to be washed frequently. This is mentioned several times in the Old Testament (see Genesis 18:4). Not washing one's feet was a sign of mourning (2 Samuel 19:24). It was considered to be the work of a slave, but Jesus washed his disciples' feet in order to emphasize the necessity of serving others (John 13).

671.

Old Testament law taught that a woman was ceremonially unclean during menstruation. The woman who touched Jesus' robe, believing it would heal her "issue of blood" (Luke 8:43), had not been able to participate in worship or community life for over 12 years.

672.

Susanna and Joanna were two women who had been healed by Jesus and took care of day-to-day tasks—laundry, sewing, and cooking—for Jesus and his followers. They helped to support Jesus and his disciples out of their own means (Luke 8:1–3).

673.

Mary of Magdalene was prominent among the women who followed Jesus. He had cast demons out of her (Luke 8:1–3), and she is mentioned more than any of the other women, including Mary, the mother of Jesus. She provided financial support for his ministry and was the first to whom Jesus appeared after his resurrection.

674.

At least four women named Mary are noted in connection with the ministry of Jesus. One, of course, was his mother. Another was Mary Magdalene, who helped fund his ministry. There was also Mary of Bethany, who, with her sister Martha, often provided a place for Jesus to stay. A fourth Mary was the mother of James and John, two of his disciples.

675.

Joseph and Mary had at least seven children (see Matthew 13:55–56). We know little about Joseph. He is generally assumed to have died before Jesus began his ministry at the age of 30, and certainly before the Crucifixion, since at that time Jesus committed the care of his mother to John.

676.

Jesus had several people who were called brothers and sisters; they may have been half brothers and sisters, stepsiblings, or possibly cousins (Matthew 12:46–47; 13:55–56). The Bible mentions Jesus' brothers a number of times and his sisters twice. His brothers included James, Joses, Simon, and Judas. His sisters are not named in the Bible.

677.

Although they have similar names, none of Jesus' brothers were apostles, but James did become the head of the church in Jerusalem.

678.

Salome was Herod's brother's daughter. She danced for Herod and upon pleasing him, received his promise to do anything for her. She asked for the head of John the Baptist on a plate, a request prompted by her mother (Matthew 14). Rather than be embarrassed in front of his guests, Herod was forced to follow through on Salome's request.

679.

Herod kept his promise to give Salome whatever she asked for. John the Baptist was beheaded in the prison and his head was delivered to her in a charger (Matthew 14:6–11 and Mark 6:21–28).

680.

A charger was a large, flat plate for carrying a joint of meat. The name comes from a word that means "to load."

681.

King Herod believed that Jesus was John the Baptist raised from the dead. He was not alone in misreading the teachings and miracles of Jesus in this way.

682.

Jesus' favorite teaching tool was the parable. In its simplest form, the parable uses a comparison to make a point. It is simple, direct, and the point is clear, such as "Again, the kingdom of heaven is like unto treasure hid in a field; the which when a man hath found, he hideth, and for joy thereof goeth and selleth all that he hath, and buyeth that field" (Matthew 13:44).

683.

Sometimes Jesus told parables to make things clear. And sometimes he told parables to make things obscure. Later, he would explain these more obscure parables to his disciples. Some of the things he taught were only for those who were seeking him and believed him (Matthew 13:1–36).

684.

Many of Jesus' parables were stories. They involved comparisons, and the characters often represented God the Father or Jesus himself. Among the most beloved extended parables are the shepherd who risks all to search for the one lost sheep, the father who eagerly takes back his wayward son, and the good Samaritan who stopped to help a robbery victim when members of society's elite would not.

685.

Jesus told about 30 parables, although some lists include as many as 50. The variance has to do with how we define a parable, since what some people label a parable others see as a simple metaphor. Generally a parable is an extended metaphor meant to illustrate a particular point, and cannot be applied more broadly.

686.

Metaphors are figures of speech in which a term describing a certain object is used to describe something else for the purpose of making a vivid comparison. This was a rhetorical device that Jesus often used. He called King Herod "that fox" (Luke 13:32). He called himself "the bread of life" (John 6:35) and "the true vine" (John 15:1). He even called some who came to follow him a "generation of vipers" (Luke 3:7).

687.

Jesus' parables may seem familiar today, but in his day, they presented revolutionary ideas using a familiar mechanism. His teachings turned the status quo on its ear. Thus the genius of the method: It imparted radical ideas in ways so simple and accessible we still learn from them today.

688.

In the Parable of the Sower, the seed that fell on rocky ground produced plants that grew but then quickly withered (Matthew 13:3–9, Mark 4:3–9, and Luke 8:5–8).

689.

In the Parable of the Mustard Seed, when the plant reached its full height, birds perched in its branches (Matthew 13:31–32, Mark 4:30–32, and Luke 13:18–19).

690.

The smallest seed mentioned in the Bible is the tiny mustard seed. The mustard plant grew into something close to five feet tall, however. Jesus used it to characterize the growth of God's kingdom, from something small (the tiny seed) to something great (the large plant), as well as to speak of the tiny amount of faith needed to work wonders.

691.

The mustard seed referred to in the Gospels was cultivated for its oil and also ground into a paste for eating or medicinal purposes.

692.

In the Parable of the Good Samaritan, the Bible does not specify the occupation of the Samaritan (Luke 10:25–37).

693.

The good Samaritan is said to have gone down from Jerusalem to Jericho. This doesn't mean that Jericho is south of Jerusalem (it's east), and it doesn't imply that Jericho was a step down from Jerusalem in wealth, urban development, or status. Jericho is 3,300 feet lower than Jerusalem, an amazing drop for a journey of only 15 miles.

694.

Few people traveled alone. Jesus tells the story of a Samaritan who cares for a man attacked by bandits, even though he was on the much-traveled road. Jesus and his disciples prudently traveled in a group.

695.

Jesus told a story about the Good Samaritan, and the woman at the well in John 4 was also a Samaritan. And when Jesus healed ten lepers and only one returned to thank him, that one was also a Samaritan. "There are not found that returned to give glory to God, save this stranger," Jesus said (Luke 17:12–19).

696.

In the Parable of the Two Sons, when their father asked them to work in the vineyard, one son agreed to work but didn't, and another said he wouldn't but did (Matthew 21:28–32).

697.

In the Parable of the Prodigal Son, the Bible doesn't specify how long it took for the prodigal son to squander his inheritance (Luke 15:11–32).

698.

Legal documents and personal letters from the first century suggest the father who waits for and welcomes the prodigal son would have been an anomaly (Luke 15:11–32). The father Jesus described was extremely gracious, since families typically cut off and ostracized any wayward children without financial recourse.

699.

The idea that God would pursue sinners to draw them back to him was revolutionary to first-century Jews. While they believed God would receive repentant sinners, they would have found the parable about a shepherd leaving 99 sheep to find a single lost sheep mystifying (Luke 15:3–7).

700.

The rabbis taught that you should forgive someone three times before you could retaliate. Peter asked Jesus how many times you had to forgive someone, thinking seven would be enough. Jesus said not seven times, but seventy times seven, or 490 times (Matthew 18:21–22).

701.

When Peter asked how many times he had to forgive someone, Jesus told the Parable of the Unmerciful Servant, where a servant who had been forgiven debt by his master demanded instant payment from someone who owed a smaller debt to him (Matthew 18:21–35).

702.

The talents in Jesus' parable of the master who gave his servants several talents were units of money. These were enormous sums of money, since the Greek *talanton* weighed between 57 and 95 pounds, and one talent was more than 15 years wages for a laborer.

703.

A talent was worth about $1,000, but a shilling, or pence, was worth about 17 cents. Jesus told a story about a man who was forgiven a debt of $10,000,000 but was unwilling to forgive someone who owed him about $17. "And his lord was wroth, and delivered him to the tormentors," Jesus said (Matthew 18:21–35).

704.

Peter probably thought that seven times was plenty. Seven symbolized completeness. Jesus, however, replied, "Until seventy times seven" (Matthew 18:21–22).

705.

In his Gospel, the Apostle John included seven miracles of Jesus from the 37 recorded in the New Testament. There were probably even more, as John writes: "And many other signs truly did Jesus in the presence of his disciples, which are not written in this book" (John 20:30).

706.

The miracle in which Jesus feeds a hungry crowd of 5,000 with five loaves and two fish is found in all the gospels. See Matthew 14:13–21, Mark 6:31–44, Luke 9:10–17, and John 6:5–15.

707.

Wherever Jesus went, crowds followed. Once, over 5,000 people gathered to hear him and after a long day were famished. One boy, who had brought a lunch, offered it to Jesus. Jesus used this meager lunch of five loaves of bread and two fish to satisfy the hungry crowd—and there were even leftovers (John 6:1–15)! While the boy was crucial to the story, we never find out his name.

708.

The term "staff of life" refers to a dietary staple, such as *bread*. Bread was the staff of life in the ancient Near East. The phrase probably comes from Leviticus 26:26, which mentions the "staff of your bread." The word bread is often used for food in the Bible. This is why, in John 6:35, Jesus refers to himself as "the bread of life."

709.

Bread and fish was the most affordable meal for common people. The disciples find loaves and fishes when feeding the 5,000, and Jesus says, "If a son shall ask bread of any of you that is a father, will he give him a stone? Or if he ask a fish, will he for a fish give him a serpent?" (Luke 11:11).

710.

Jesus fed a crowd of 4,000 with seven loaves and a few fish, with seven baskets left over. This is related as a separate event from the feeding of the 5,000 with five loaves of two fish (Matthew 15:32–39 and Mark 8:1–10).

711.

Matthew wrote that Jesus fed a crowd of 5,000 with bread and fish, and another time he says Jesus fed a crowd of 4,000 with bread and fish. Both stories are true because each was a separate incident. Not only are the numbers different, but so are the places, as well as the amount of food they started with and collected afterward (Matthew 14:14–21 and 15:32–39).

712.

After the feeding of the 5,000, who were mostly Jews, the leftovers filled 12 baskets, corresponding with the 12 tribes of Israel. After feeding the 4,000 in the more Gentile region east of the Jordan, they took up seven baskets, in reference to the seven heathen peoples (Deuteronomy 7:1; Acts 13:19).

713.

After Jesus fed the multitudes, the Pharisees and Sadducees asked him for a "sign from heaven." Jesus said that the only sign the people would receive was the "sign of the prophet Jonas" (Matthew 16:4). The sign of Jonas, or Jonah, is the conversion of Nineveh, a pagan city. His ministry and several specific miracles reflected this openness to non-Jewish peoples.

714.

Just as Jonah had been in the fish's belly for three days and nights, so Jesus would be in the grave for the same amount of time. Jesus' appearance after the three days would indict his generation, just as Jonah's appearance in Nineveh after three days indicted the Ninevites.

715.

A house was thoroughly cleaned on the day before Passover, and all the bread made with yeast (leavened) was eaten or burned. There had to be a fresh start. Jesus used this idea when warning his disciples about the "leaven" of the Pharisees (Matthew 16:6). His kingdom would require a completely new way of thinking.

716.

Each morning during the seven-day Feast of Tabernacles, a procession of barefoot priests would go to the Pool of Siloam in the Kidron Valley and bring a pitcher of water back to the temple and pour it into the base of the altar, chanting, "With joy you will draw water from the wells of salvation." During this ritual, the crowd would wave palm branches and chant the Hallel (Psalms 113–118).

717.

In the course of a debate with a group of Jews, Jesus claimed to have seen Abraham. When they challenged this statement, he replied, "Before Abraham was, I am" (John 8:58). The Jews were enraged with this reference to "I am," since only God was to be referred to in this way. They considered this blasphemy, and tried to stone Jesus to death. This is one of the most direct statements in the Gospels equating Jesus with God.

718.

Jesus is intentional about his use of the phrase "I am," a reference to the name God gave himself when speaking to Moses (Exodus 3:14). Jesus often uses this phrase in describing himself and says "I am" the good shepherd, the door, the light, the bread, the way, the truth, the life, and the resurrection.

719.

On the last day of one year's Feast of Tabernacles festival, Jesus stood and cried out, "If any man thirst, let him come unto me, and drink" (John 7:37).

720.

In Matthew's gospel, the king in the Parable of the Great Banquet was throwing a banquet for his son's wedding. Luke's gospel also contains a version of the parable, but he tells of a "great man" instead of a king, and the reason for the banquet isn't given.

721.

On her wedding day, a bride waited with her friends at her home until her husband and his friends arrived and took her back to his parents' house. Celebrants danced and poured oil and perfume on the couple, scattering nuts and grain on the ground. Jesus used this image in the parable of the wise and foolish virgins (Matthew 25:1–13).

722.

Jesus talked a lot about money. In fact, he talked about it more often than he talked about heaven or hell. He told 38 parables, and 16 of them dealt with how to handle or think about our possessions and our wealth. While there are about 500 verses in the Bible about prayer, there are over 2,000 about money—most are cautionary.

723.

Many Jewish women strung together coins from their dowry and wore them around their neck. When Jesus told the parable of the woman who lost a coin, the coin may have been such an heirloom, with as much sentimental value as monetary value. This explains her panic and determination to find the coin. (See Luke 15:8–10).

724.

The story of the rich man and a beggar named Lazarus (Luke 16:19–31) is the only story Jesus told in which he named one of the characters. This suggests that this story really happened, and was not just an illustration. Jesus did not name the rich man, but tradition says his name was Dives.

725.

When a man in the crowd wanted Jesus to tell the man's brother to share a family inheritance, Jesus responded by telling the crowd the Parable of the Rich Fool, which illustrated the dangers of concentrating on earthly wealth instead of our relationship with God.

726.

In the Parable of the Pharisee and the Tax Collector, the Pharisee bragged about giving a tenth of his income to God, also known as a tithe (Luke 18:10–14).

727.

A mina was an amount of money worth about one hundred days' wages. Jesus told a parable about a king who left this amount to ten servants when he was called away (Luke 19:11–27). The servant with the best return on the money he was given to invest produced ten minas—quite a sum!

728.

In Galilee, Jesus encountered a deaf man with a speech impediment. Taking him aside, Jesus put his fingers in the man's ears, and he "spat and touched his tongue." Looking upward, Jesus said something that sounded like "*Effatha*." The Aramaic word for "open" is *pthah*, and its passive imperative would have been *ethpthah*. "And straightway his ears were opened, and the string of his tongue was loosed, and he spake plain" (Mark 7:35).

729.

Mark 8:22–26 describes Jesus healing a blind man with spit: "And he took the blind man by the hand, and led him out of the town; and when he had spit on his eyes, and put his hands upon him, he asked him if he saw ought" (Mark 8:23).

730.

Mark speaks of only one person whom Jesus healed by increments, a blind man from Bethsaida (Mark 8:22–25). Jesus appeared to be illustrating the principle that belief is not a sudden recognition, but a process by which one comes to a deeper understanding. He had just asked his disciples in verse 18, "Having eyes, see ye not?"

731.

Jesus only healed people who asked for his help. For example, he specifically asked blind Bartimaeus what he wanted Jesus to do (Mark 10:46–52). He also frequently commended the faith of those who asked, such as the hemorrhaging woman: "Daughter, be of good comfort; thy faith hath made thee whole" (Matthew 9:22).

732.

When one gentile woman asked Jesus to heal her daughter, he said, "It is not meet to take the children's bread, and to cast it to dogs" (Matthew 15:26). Some say Jesus was teasing this woman, and others that he was mocking his disciples who often felt as though they should have nothing to do with gentiles. Jesus healed her daughter and then went on to heal many gentiles in the Decapolis east of Galilee.

733.

On two occasions a voice from heaven described Jesus as "my beloved son": at the beginning of his ministry when he was baptized and near the end of his ministry on the Mount of Transfiguration. He never referred to himself as the Son of God, but he often spoke of God as his Father.

734.

Peter, James, and John witnessed Jesus' transfiguration (Matthew 17:1, Mark 9:2, and Luke 9:28).

735.

Moses and Elijah appeared with Jesus at the transfiguration (Matthew 17:1–4, Mark 9:2–5, and Luke 9:27–33).

736.

There were 70 elders that assisted Moses in governing ancient Israel, and there were 70 members of the ruling council in Jesus' day, the Sanhedrin. Jesus sent 70 disciples, in groups of two, to teach and heal in Judea. Since Jesus was not as well known there, this may have been a much tougher audience than those in Galilee who had seen his miracles. (See Luke 10:1–3.)

737.

Scorpions are mentioned many times in the Bible, always as threats the Israelites faced or as symbols of great pain and hardship. Jesus appointed 70 followers to whom he gave authority to "tread on serpents and scorpions. . . and nothing shall by any means hurt you" (Luke 10:19).

738.

After Jesus sent out the 70 disciples, Luke uses the word *myrias* to describe the crowds that flocked to hear Jesus in the last six months of his ministry. The word means "tens of thousands," and suggests the throngs that gathered were larger than even in Galilee, where Jesus spent most of his ministry.

739.

The word *Lucifer* appears only once in the Bible. Latin for "light bringer," it is used in Isaiah 14:12 to refer to the king of Babylon and mock his fall from power: "How art thou fallen from heaven, O Lucifer, son of the morning!" Because Christians associated this passage with Jesus saying "I beheld Satan as lightning fall from heaven" (Luke 10:18), the name Lucifer became another name for Satan.

740.

Peter's name in Greek (*Petros*) means "rock" (*petra*). A climactic point in Jesus' ministry came when Peter confessed that Jesus was the Messiah, the Son of God. Jesus blessed him and said, "Thou art Peter [*Petros*], and upon this rock [*petra*] I will build my church" (Matthew 16:18).

741.

Jesus told Peter that "I will give unto thee the keys of the kingdom of heaven: and whatsoever thou shalt bind on earth shall be bound in heaven" (Matthew 16:19). This was a statement of the authority he received.

742.

"Get thee behind me, Satan" was the rebuke Jesus directed at Peter when he was speaking of the suffering that Jesus was to undergo, and Peter objected that this should not occur (Matthew 16:23). The effect of Peter's words was to tempt Jesus to abandon his mission, and he rebuked Peter in similar terms that he had done earlier with Satan himself (Matthew 4:10).

743.

The annual temple tax on Jewish men was a half shekel, equal to about two days' pay. When Peter spoke to Jesus about paying taxes, Jesus sent him out to catch a fish (Matthew 17:24–27). Jesus said the fish would have a large shekel coin in its mouth—enough to pay the annual tax for both of them.

744.

The fish with a shekel coin in its mouth was probably the tilapia, a fish commonly found in the Sea of Galilee. This fish has a large mouth in which it carries its eggs, and it is often called St. Peter's Fish.

745.

Before he died, Jesus spent time "by the farther side of Jordan" where the influence of the Essenes was the strongest. Here he was asked about divorce because it was controversial: The Pharisees taught that divorce was permissible, but the Essenes did not. He sided with the Essenes on this issue (Mark 10:1–9).

746.

Jesus was familiar with the Essenes, a group of priests who withdrew from temple worship in the second century B.C. and rejected the high priests in Jerusalem as pagans. The Essenes did not offer sacrifices but purified themselves in ritual baths. It is thought that Jesus' cousin John the Baptist lived with this group for several years.

747.

Jesus was tough on the rich, perhaps most famously in Matthew 19:16–24, when a wealthy young man tells Jesus he's been keeping the commandments scrupulously, yet still feels he's lacking something. "Jesus said unto him, If thou wilt be perfect, go and sell that thou hast, and give to the poor, and thou shalt have treasure in heaven: and come and follow me."

748.

Jesus used hyperbole when he said, "It is easier for a camel to go through the eye of a needle, than for a rich man to enter into the kingdom of God" (Mark 10:25).

749.

Jesus used the image of a camel going through the eye of a needle to explain how difficult it is for some to enter the kingdom of God (Matthew 19:24). Some say this refers to a small pedestrian gate in the city wall that was so small a camel could only get through it on its knees. But the Greek word used means a literal tailor's needle, and there is no literary evidence that the gate was referred to in this way.

750.

Jesus left Galilee about three months before his death in Jerusalem. He traveled to Perea, a small town near where he was baptized about three years earlier; Bethany, where he raised Lazarus from the dead; and Jericho, where he called Zacchaeus down from a tree.

751.

In ancient Israel, olive oil was used as food, fuel, and as a grooming product. When a host welcomed a guest into his home, he would almost always anoint his head as a sign of respect. Indeed, one of the most famous stories in the New Testament is of Jesus being anointed by an unnamed woman in Mark 14:3–9: "She hath done what she could: she is come aforehand to anoint my body to the burying."

752.

At Bethany, a woman anointed Jesus with costly perfume in a container of alabaster (Matthew 26:7, Mark 14:3, and Luke 7:37). While John's gospel account doesn't specify a material, unlike the other gospels it does name the woman as Mary, sister of Martha and Lazarus (John 12:2–8).

753.

Mary and Martha were the names of Lazarus' sisters. Jesus loved all three siblings (John 11:1–5).

754.

Nard was a very expensive perfume imported from India. This was the perfume that Mary of Bethany poured on Jesus' feet and wiped off with her hair (John 12:1–8).

755.

When Jesus and his followers visited the town of Bethany, they stayed with sisters Martha and Mary (Luke 10). Their brother Lazarus is not specifically mentioned, though he may have been there as well. Martha is described as welcoming Jesus in "her house," suggesting she was the owner and possibly the oldest of the three siblings. Her name actually means "lady" or "mistress."

756.

Lazarus had been buried for four days when Jesus came to Bethany to raise him from the dead (John 11:17).

757.

When Jesus saw how troubled Mary and Martha were when their brother Lazarus died, the Bible says he "groaned in the spirit."

758.

The Bible's shortest verse is John 11:35, "Jesus wept." This happened when Jesus heard that his friend Lazarus had died, so he performed a miracle and brought Lazarus back from the dead.

759.

At the raising of Lazarus, Jesus uttered a rather strange prayer for the benefit of the crowd. He said, "Father, I thank thee that thou hast heard me. And I knew that thou hearest me always: but because of the people which stand by I said it, that they may believe that thou hast sent me." (John 11:41–42). This miracle was a demonstration of his identity, and this prayer makes that clear.

760.

By the time Jesus arrived in Bethany to stay with Mary and Martha the week before he died, the Sanhedrin had already issued orders for his arrest. John tells us that their brother Lazarus, whom Jesus raised from the dead, was added to the list of those to be eliminated (John 12:9–11).

761.

The Roman Senate farmed out the collection of taxes to entrepreneurs, usually from the privileged classes. These investors would hire a "magister" to oversee a five-year contract, and they would hire and oversee tax collectors who were encouraged to charge as much as possible. These are referred to as "publicans" in the New Testament, and Jesus made friends with some of them—most notably Matthew, one of his disciples, and Zacchaeus, well-known for fraud.

762.

In ancient Israel, tax collectors were considered traitors by their fellow Jews. That is why Jews were so appalled at Jesus' casual attitude toward taxes. He also socialized with tax collectors. One of them, a man named Zacchaeus who had been skimming from the taxes he collected, repented of his ways after Jesus dined in his home. Zacchaeus promised before the Lord to give half of his goods to the poor and to restore any man he cheated fourfold (Luke 19:8).

763.

No short person's height is actually given, but Zacchaeus was noted for his short stature. Luke 19 tells us that when Jesus came to town, Zacchaeus climbed a sycamore tree to see him because he (Zacchaeus) was too short to see over the crowd.

764.

Over a third of the Gospel of John describes the week between Palm Sunday and the Resurrection. It begins after Mary anointed Jesus with costly perfume (John 12).

765.

In Christian tradition, the Sunday before Easter has come to be known as Palm Sunday. This was because people welcomed Jesus into Jerusalem by spreading leafy branches on the road before his donkey as he was entering the city at the time of the Passover (in the spring). The cutting of palm branches was usually practiced in the fall, at the Festival of Tabernacles, as part of the construction of the booths (Leviticus 23:40–42).

766.

In early Christian art and on Christian tombs, images of palms represented martyrs. Those who died for the faith frequently were portrayed as holding palm leaves. Using traditional symbolism, their victory was shown to be one over death and into newness of life.

767.

The date palm can live for 200 years, and along with other types of palms in the region, it provided wax, sugar, dyes, and resin. It became a symbol of the righteous enjoying well-deserved prosperity, which partly explains the expectation of the crowds who lined the street waving palm leaves as Jesus entered Jerusalem. They wanted Jesus to become king and overthrow the Romans, ushering in a new age of prosperity.

768.

Jesus rode a donkey colt into Jerusalem. Matthew suggests there were two animals, however, a mother and a colt (Matthew 21:2–7). The mother may have been brought along to keep the colt calm.

769.

Several passages in the Old Testament speak of a king riding on a donkey. This is most striking in Zechariah 9:9, where it is prophesied that a king comes triumphant and victorious yet riding humbly on a donkey. Jesus' entrance into Jerusalem fulfilled this prophecy (Matthew 21:5). The use of a donkey instead of a horse emphasized the peaceful nature of the king.

770.

An essential part of Hebrew attire was a cloak, an outer garment worn like a sport coat or jacket. It was little more than a square cloth with a hole for one's head. The color and quality varied, however, and it could be used as collateral, provided it was returned to the owner by night so he or she could use it as a blanket. This is the garment people spread along the street when Jesus entered Jerusalem.

771.

Jesus freely came and went in the Temple and its courtyards. Under the colonnades of the outer court, the Jewish scribes and Pharisees taught the Law and held their debates. It was here that the 12-year-old Jesus impressed these rabbis with his knowledge. It was also here that an angry Jesus overturned the tables of the moneychangers and the merchants because they had turned God's house into "a den of thieves."

772.

The ruling class, the elders, was made up of mostly wealthy and powerful families, but by the time of Jesus a new elite was beginning to arise—the Scribes. The Scribes came from all walks of life to study under famous rabbis for 25 years before they were ordained at the age of 40. The Pharisees, on the other hand, were not known for their study as much as for following the teachings of the Scribes.

773.

The profit from the market booths in the temple area went to enrich the family of the high priest. Jesus drove out the moneychangers and merchants twice, once at the very beginning of his ministry and again on the Monday before his death. "My house shall be called a house of prayer," he said, "but ye have made it a den of thieves" (Matthew 21:13).

774.

Jesus drove the money changers out of the temple because they were overcharging the people. Adult men had to pay a half shekel each year to help maintain the temple—about two days' wages. To do this, foreign money had to be exchanged into official temple money, and the exchange rate was as high as 8:1.

775.

Some Pharisees tried to trap Jesus by asking him whether they should pay taxes to Caesar. If he said yes, they could accuse him of neglecting God's way. If he said no, he could be accused of subversion of Roman law. Jesus frustrated them by simply showing them a coin with Caesar's likeness on it and stating, "Render to Caesar the things that are Caesar's, and to God the things that are God's" (Mark 12:17).

776.

The coin Jesus referred to when he said, "Render therefore unto Caesar the things which are Caesar's" was probably a denarius (Matthew 22:21). This small, silver Roman coin was equivalent to a laborer's wage for a day's work. The "widow's mite" he noticed in the temple was likely a lepton, the coin of least value at that time.

777.

Jesus saw a poor widow dropping two small copper coins into the treasury boxes in the Temple. These were the smallest coins in circulation, worth less than a penny, and yet they were the last things she owned (Mark 12:44).

778.

When a widow dropped two "mites" into the treasury at the temple, Jesus said she had actually given more than all the rich men who paraded their wealth and dumped in fortunes. "She of her want did cast in all that she had," he said (Mark 12:44).

779.

At the height of his popularity, Jesus was grilled by interviewers sent by his enemies. "Master, which is the great commandment in the law?" they challenged. Jesus' reply was brilliant. "Thou shalt love the Lord thy God with all thy heart, and with all thy soul, and with all thy mind." Then he added—"Thou shalt love thy neighbour as thyself"—declaring that all the scriptures hang on these two laws (Matthew 22:36–40).

780.

Jesus knew he was going to die in Jerusalem, and mentioned it at least three times (Mark 8:31; 9:31; 10:33–34; and parallel passages in other Gospels). He went to Jerusalem to "give his life a ransom for many" (Matthew 20:28).

781.

Talking to a crowd about his impending suffering, Jesus wondered whether he should ask his Father to avoid it. But he concluded, "but for this cause came I unto this hour." And then he prayed: "Father, glorify thy name." A voice from heaven replied, "I have both glorified it, and will glorify it again." Some thought it was just thunder, but Jesus explained, "This voice came not because of me, but for your sakes" (John 12:27–30).

782.

When Jesus told his disciples that he "must" die, he used a word that means something is legally or morally binding. *Dei* is used more than 100 times in the New Testament to refer to or indicate necessity imposed by the will of God. Jesus' trip to the cross was deliberate and calculated. (See Matthew 16:21.)

783.

In one sermon Jesus told six stories in a row about being ready for his return (see Matthew 24–25). These stories emphasize being alert, faithful, and busy. Here we are specifically told to care for the poor and powerless.

784.

People often put tents on their roofs for the Feast of Tabernacles, when they lived for a week in temporary shelters to remind themselves of their time in the wilderness. Wealthier families started to build more permanent structures on their roofs, which eventually became second stories. Jesus held the last supper in one of these upstairs chambers.

785.

While all four gospels tell the story of the Lord's supper, only John tells of Jesus washing the feet of the disciples as part of it (John 13:4–12). John's account of the Lord's Supper, in which Jesus talks to his disciples extensively, is significantly longer than that of the other gospels.

786.

Banquet guests typically bathed before arriving, and only their feet needed to be washed before dinner. When Jesus washed his disciples' feet at the Last Supper, Peter asked Jesus to wash his hands and head as well, but Jesus said it wasn't necessary (John 13:10). Hand washing would also be part of the dinner experience.

787.

Washing the feet of guests was common in the dry, dusty climate of Palestine, although it was usually done by slaves or servants, or sometimes women or children. Abraham offered this gesture to an angel, as did Abigail to King David, and a prostitute to Jesus.

788.

At festival dinners, people reclined on a three-sided couch, called a triclinium, with their feet stretched out away from the table. At the Last Supper, the disciples argued about who would share the couch at the head of the table with Jesus (Luke 22:24).

789.

The Last Supper was a Passover meal Jesus shared with his disciples on the night he was arrested. From scripture and tradition, the Passover had developed a distinct menu and liturgy, and we see hints of that in the Gospels' account of the Last Supper. Along with Judas, Jesus dips his (unleavened) bread in the dip (which represented the mortar the Israelites used as slaves).

790.

Stews were very common in Jesus' day, but spoons were rare. Diners would scoop food out of a common pot with bread. It was considered rude to dip in at the same time as someone else—something that happened with Jesus and Judas at the Last Supper (Mark 14:18–20).

791.

No Jewish meal was complete without bread. Before the meal, the father would break the bread and give thanks, passing it around to everyone before the other food was served. A separate blessing was offered for the rest of the meal. This is what was going on at the Last Supper when Jesus first gave thanks, broke the bread, and passed it to his disciples, telling them to "this do in remembrance of me" (Luke 22:19).

792.

Old Testament law clearly taught that drinking or eating blood was absolutely forbidden. Even though he was speaking figuratively, Jesus' listeners would have been shocked and repulsed when he said, "Whoso eateth my flesh, and drinketh my blood, hath eternal life" (John 6:54).

793.

Jesus instituted the Lord's Supper for his disciples during a Passover meal. Christians believe that the Passover, when a sacrificial lamb was eaten, had been pointing toward Christ's own sacrifice for 14 centuries at the time he ate it with his disciples. The day Jesus died lambs were still being slain in the temple.

794.

John's Gospel contains a lengthy account of Jesus' teaching and conversation during the Last Supper. He also includes a prayer Jesus prayed at that time. At one point he even prays for us, specifically. "Neither pray I for these alone, but for them also which shall believe on me through their word" (John 17:20).

795.

In John 17, Jesus prays for his disciples before he dies, a prayer sometimes referred to as the "High Priestly" prayer; it follows the pattern of the prayer offered by the high priest on the Day of Atonement. Others think of it as the Lord's Prayer, since it reflects Jesus' own heart, and think of the other, well-known prayer by that name as the "Model" prayer.

796.

Both Mark and Matthew describe Jesus and his disciples singing a hymn at the end of the Lord's Supper, before going to the Mount of Olives (Matthew 26:30 and Mark 14:26).

797.

Jesus crossed the Cedron brook on the night that he was betrayed by Judas (John 18:1).

798.

Before his crucifixion, Jesus went to the Garden of Gethsemane to pray. *Gethsemane* comes from an Aramaic word meaning "oil press." The Garden of Gethsemane today still has many very old olive trees.

799.

Averaging 26 to 49 feet in height, an olive tree is short and squat—about the size of an apple tree. Though olive trees do not bear fruit until they are 15 years old, they live for hundreds of years; in fact, an olive tree in Algarve, Portugal, has been radiocarbon dated at 2,000 years old. This means that it is possible that there are olive trees in Israel that have been alive since the time of Christ!

800.

The Mount of Olives was outside the walls of Jerusalem, near the eastern wall of the temple. It is hard to know exactly what the city looked like, but the first-century Jewish historian Josephus said that when you came over the top of the mountain, the temple looked like a snow-capped mountain—gleaming white buildings trimmed in gold.

801.

Passover is also called *Leil Shimurim*, night of the watchers. This refers to Exodus 12:42. This was the same night Jesus prayed in the Garden of Gethsemane, asking his disciples to keep watch. "Couldest not thou watch one hour?" he asked Peter (Mark 14:37–38).

802.

The book of Hebrews says that Jesus learned "obedience by the things which he suffered" (5:8). Some consider Jesus the ultimate "free" man, but repeatedly he is said to be "in submission" to the Father. In Gethsemane, he asked his Father to "let this cup pass from me" (Matthew 26:39), but the Father decreed that he should die for our sins, and he went to the cross willingly.

803.

Singing is common in the Bible, and the early church was commanded to do it (see Ephesians 5:19). The book of Psalms is in fact a book of hymns, used for thousands of years by Jews. Jesus himself sang at least once. After the Lord's Supper, before Jesus and his disciples traveled to the Garden of Gethsemane, both Matthew and Mark tell us, "And when they had sung an hymn, they went out" (Matthew 26:30; Mark 14:26).

804.

Jesus used the Aramaic word *abba*, an intimate form of the word *ab*, which means "father" when he prayed in the Garden of Gethsemane. It was an informal term of intimacy and respect used by children, similar to our use of "Daddy." Jesus used this term in Mark 14:36 to describe the intimacy that believers could have with God the Father. Apostle Paul says that as adopted children all believers can think of God in this way (Romans 8:15).

805.

The Gospel of Mark is the only one of the four gospels to mention the episode of a young man who escaped naked from the Garden of Gethsemane at Jesus' arrest (Mark 14:51–52). The details seem too autobiographical for the reference to not be the book's author—Mark himself.

806.

Some six different people in the New Testament were named Judas. One was a brother of Jesus (Matthew 13:55) and he wrote the book of Jude. Another Judas was a disciple of Jesus. To distinguish that Judas from Judas Iscariot, John 14:22 calls him "not Iscariot."

807.

When Judas Iscariot betrayed Jesus to the Jewish authorities, he was given 30 pieces of silver in payment. This has led to the phrase "blood money," which is money received in exchange for the life of a human being.

808.

30 pieces of silver was a ridiculously low sum. In the Old Testament, this was the sum to be paid if a man's ox gored a slave. This reflects the low esteem in which Jesus was held by Judas and the Jewish leaders.

809.

When Judas came to betray Jesus, officials were expecting a fight. Judas was accompanied by a "detachment," at least 200 troops, in the middle of the night (John 18:3). "Be ye come out, as against a thief, with swords and staves?" Jesus asked (Luke 22:52).

810.

Emperor Augustus reorganized the Roman army into legions of 6,000 men. These were broken down into "centuries" of 100 men, which were grouped into "cohorts" of 600 men. During the life of Christ there were probably only a few cohorts stationed in Israel. When Jesus was arrested, he said his Father could put more than 12 legions of angels at his disposal (Matthew 26:53).

811.

Jesus did not save his miraculous healing powers only for those who believed in him. Malchus, the servant of the high priest, was with the group of soldiers who came to arrest Jesus. Peter struck him with a sword, severing his ear. But Jesus said, "Suffer ye thus far" and healed Malchus' ear (Luke 22:51).

812.

According to the Gospel of Matthew, Judas returned the thirty pieces of silver (before hanging himself), and the elders used it to buy a potter's field—a small plot filled with broken pottery and other trash that would be used to bury poor people (Matthew 27:3–10).

813.

Akeldama was the Aramaic name, meaning "field of blood," given to the field bought with the 30 pieces of silver that Judas received when he betrayed Jesus. The name seems to be due to two reasons: the spilling of Judas' blood (Acts 1:18–19), and the fact that the field was bought with "blood money" (from Jesus' betrayal) (Matthew 27:6).

814.

"Judas Tree" is the name given to a tree that Judas supposedly hung himself from (Matthew 27:5). It has reddish flowers that look like drops of blood. The flowers appear before the leaves, and spring straight out of the trunk itself. The tree is the *Cercis siliquastrum*. Tradition states that the tree weeps blood each spring in memory of Judas.

815.

Jesus was arrested and taken to Annas, the father-in-law of the high priest, Caiaphas. Annas had been the high priest until he was fired by the Romans in A.D. 15, but was still considered to be the power behind the throne. The Jews accepted this, since the high priest was supposed to be appointed for life.

816.

Annas interrogated Jesus, but by law the accused was not to be questioned by the judge. Everything was determined on the testimony of witnesses. Jesus was well within his legal rights to ask Annas, "Why askest thou me? Ask them which heard me, what I have said unto them" (John 18:21).

817.

Antonia was a fortress that overlooked the temple, built by Herod the Great and named after Mark Antony. Although the temple area was governed by the priests, the fortress was an ever-present reminder of Roman power and authority. Jesus was tried and then scourged here before Pontius Pilate.

818.

Pontius Pilate was a shrewd and hot-tempered Roman aristocrat who was the Roman governor of Judea from A.D. 26 to 36. His rule was marked by much civil unrest, and he was finally removed for excessive brutality in putting down occasional uprisings in the province. The Jews brought Jesus to trial before Pilate because they were not allowed to execute a prisoner without his permission.

819.

Pilate pronounced judgment on Jesus at a place called the Pavement (in Hebrew, *Gabbatha*) (John 19:13). This was probably in the Antonia, a massive fortress built by Herod which was at the northwest corner of the Temple Mount. Paul was also imprisoned there. A large stone pavement, more than 150 feet square, can be seen today under a convent in this area.

820.

At Jesus' trial, when Pontius Pilate heard Jesus was from Galilee, he sent him to King Herod, who was visiting Jerusalem at that time. Herod had heard of Jesus and wanted him to do a miracle, but Jesus refused. In fact, he wouldn't even speak to him. (See Luke 23:6–12.)

821.

When Jesus was tried before Pontius Pilate, a notorious criminal, Barabbas, was in Roman custody. He was released when Jesus was sentenced to death (Matthew 27:16–26, Mark 15:15, Luke 23:18–24, and John 18:39–40).

822.

Pilate failed in his attempt to free Jesus and freed Barabbas instead. Christians have long seen themselves in Barabbas: a guilty man set free because an innocent man died in his place. Appropriately, his name has a generic meaning that could apply to anyone: "son of the father."

823.

The Roman governor Pilate washed his hands at Jesus' arraignment to symbolize his withdrawal from responsibility for whatever might happen to Jesus (Matthew 27:24). This practice was not new. The Old Testament has many examples of ritual hand washing to symbolize innocence (Psalm 26:6 and Deuteronomy 21:6–8).

824.

Although Joseph of Arimathea and Nicodemus were members of the ruling council, the Sanhedrin, apparently neither of them were present at the trial of Jesus. It is supposed that they were not invited because they were known Jesus sympathizers. Joseph is described as "a disciple of Jesus, but secretly" (John 19:38).

825.

Before Jesus was crucified, he knew his disciples would desert him and quoted Zechariah 13:7: "Smite the shepherd, and the sheep shall be scattered." These same disciples gathered in Jerusalem after the resurrection and started the first church. Then they scattered to preach to the rest of the known world.

826.

Jesus was crucified at a place called Golgotha. The name Golgotha means place of a skull (Matthew 27:33, Mark 15:22, John 19:17).

827.

Crucifixion was normally reserved for the lower classes in Greek and Roman societies. It was a humiliating and excruciatingly slow, painful death. Prisoners were normally whipped until blood flowed, then they were either tied or nailed to the cross and left to die of gradual suffocation.

828.

When Roman soldiers flogged a prisoner in preparation for crucifixion, the victim was tied to a pole or beam so he would not fall down—even if he lost consciousness. They used a whip with leather strands, tied at points into knots that held pieces of metal and bone. The idea was to lash with the whip and then rip it sideways, tearing the flesh of the victim as much as possible.

829.

Blood represented life in the Bible, and shed blood represented death. The sacrifice for sin required the shedding of blood. This was true whether the victim was an innocent animal or the ultimate sacrificial lamb, Jesus.

830.

Although he was poor, Jesus had an expensive tunic—one with no seams, woven out of a single piece of cloth. It was probably a gift. The soldiers who crucified him decided not to tear it, but to cast dice for it (John 19:24).

831.

According to John 19:23, Jesus' tunic "was without seam, woven from the top throughout." Most looms of Jesus' time produced cloth that was about three feet wide, so two panels had to be sewn together to make a tunic. But the looms in Galilee were wide enough to weave a tunic in one piece, making Jesus' seamless tunic more valuable.

832.

Roman soldiers gave Jesus a drink from a sponge while he was on the cross. Sponges are marine animals whose skeletons provide the familiar sponge. The Roman writer Pliny states that it was standard practice for Roman soldiers to carry a sponge with them to use in getting themselves a drink, precisely in the way that the Gospels describe.

833.

The gospels of Matthew, Mark, and Luke tell of the incident where Simon of Cyrene was pressed into service to help Jesus carry the cross up to Golgotha.

834.

Simon of Cyrene had two sons who were apparently known to the early church. Mark 15:21 says Simon was the father of Alexander and Rufus, as if the readers of the Gospel would know those two men.

835.

Very little detail is given about the incident in terms of Simon of Cyrene's history or his response to the incident. See Matthew 27:32, Mark 15:21, and Luke 23:26.

836.

All four Gospels state that a plaque was placed on Jesus' cross identifying him. The letters "INRI," often seen on this plaque in paintings of Jesus' crucifixion, represent the Latin words for the phrase, "Jesus of Nazareth, King of the Jews."

837.

John 19:20 states that the plaque on Jesus' cross was written in three languages. Hebrew was the local language, Greek was the language of commerce, and Latin was the language of the Roman Empire. When the Roman Empire became Christianized, Latin became the language of the church.

838.

Several women at Jesus' Crucifixion were wailing in grief, but he urged them not to grieve him but their own children. "For if they do these things in a green tree, what shall be done in the dry?" he said, citing a proverb (Luke 23:31). He was saying that if God pours out his wrath on his own Son, what will he do with those who rejected him?

839.

Only one of the 12 disciples was at the cross when Jesus died. All the rest had fled, but John—the youngest of the disciples—was there.

840.

Even a crucified man had the right to make a verbal will, even from the cross. Jesus used the formula of Jewish family law to fulfill his obligation to his mother by transferring it to his disciple John. Jesus asked that John look after his mother, saying, "behold thy son" to Mary and "behold thy mother" to John. John took Mary into his own home (John 19:26–27).

841.

Jesus' crucifixion followed typical Roman procedures. He was publicly whipped, forced to carry his own cross, and nailed to it. A tablet identifying him was attached above his head. The book of John states (19:36) that this fulfilled an Old Testament prophecy.

842.

While on the cross, Jesus cried, "*Eli, Eli, lema sabachthani?*" This is Hebrew for, "My God, my God, why have you forsaken me?" Some bystanders thought he was calling for Elijah; however, this is actually the first verse of Psalm 22, which contains an eerily accurate description of the process of crucifixion (though it was written centuries before the Romans invented crucifixion).

843.

Jesus was on the cross for about six or seven hours, from mid-morning to late afternoon. Sometimes it could take three or four days to die on a cross, but Jesus had been tried and tortured for hours before his Crucifixion. But John says he died when he was ready: "he bowed his head, and gave up the ghost" (John 19:30).

844.

The actual cause of death by crucifixion was asphyxiation. A block was provided for the victim's feet, however, allowing them to push their body up to catch a breath, thus prolonging the agony. Since the Passover was approaching, the soldiers came around to break each victim's legs so they would die more quickly, but Jesus was already dead (John 19:31–34).

845.

The Romans typically crucified people near a highway, so this would have been seen by Jewish people from many countries as they were streaming into Jerusalem for the Passover.

846.

The total time Jesus was dead was not much more than 36 hours. According to the Gospels, Jesus died on a Friday afternoon, about 3:00 p.m. He was placed in a tomb that evening and remained there until sometime early Sunday morning, before the women got there.

847.

The Jews and Romans did not have or use zero in their calculations and began adding with one. This explains how Jesus was dead "three days," when it was only a day and a half from Friday afternoon to Sunday morning.

848.

Not all Pharisees were hostile to Jesus. Some of them even warned him to leave Jerusalem because of the plot to kill him (Luke 13:31).

849.

Two Pharisees, Nicodemus and Joseph of Arimathea, took personal and political risks to care for his body after he was crucified. (Matthew 27:57–58, Mark 15:43–44, Luke 23:50–52, and John 19:38).

850.

Joseph of Arimathea (a village in Judea) was a wealthy member of the Sanhedrin who came forward and offered his own tomb for Jesus' burial (Luke 23:50–56).

851.

Dead bodies were well cared for in all ancient societies. In the New Testament, we see examples of corpses being washed, anointed with aromatic preparations, and wrapped in linen cloths or bandages with a separate face cloth. Lack of burial was the ultimate humiliation. The evil queen Jezebel was left in the street and her flesh eaten by the dogs.

852.

The body of Jesus was wrapped in strips of linen mixed with spices—probably myrrh and aloes—designed to inhibit odors during decay. When Jesus asked that the stone be removed from Lazarus' tomb, his sister Martha was concerned about the smell (John 11:39).

853.

An executed criminal could not be buried in his family's tomb until a year after his death, and no public mourning or funeral possession was allowed. A few women went to the tomb of Jesus, but no public rituals were conducted for him and he was not buried in a family tomb.

854.

After a funeral, the tomb was often painted white to warn others that a body was decaying there. When it was fully decayed, the bones were collected and put in a stone box so the tomb could be used again. Jesus once referred to the Pharisees as "whited sepulchres" (Matthew 23:27).

855.

Only one day of the week had a name, the Sabbath. The day before the Sabbath was sometimes called the Day of Preparation, but days were usually numbered. Matthew, for example, says the resurrection occurred on the "first day of the week" (Matthew 28:1).

856.

The Bible recounts 12 different occasions when Jesus appeared to his followers after his resurrection. Once he even fixed breakfast for them: Fish were roasting over a fire as they came in from their boats after fishing all night (John 21:9). On another occasion he ate with them, proving he was not a ghost (Luke 24:41–43).

857.

Jesus appeared to his disciples several times after his resurrection, but they didn't always realize it was him at first. Mary Magdalene thought he was a gardener and didn't recognize him until he called her name (John 20:14–16). Two disciples on the road to Emmaus didn't know him until he prayed (Luke 24:13–35).

858.

In one post-Resurrection appearance, Jesus came to his disciples after they had a night of unsuccessful fishing and told them to throw their net to the right side. They gathered 153 fish in their nets when they did as he said (John 21:1–14).

859.

The disciple Thomas is often referred to as "doubting Thomas," since he insisted on seeing the wounds after Jesus was resurrected. But he was actually the first to understand that Jesus would die—and also volunteered to die with him. He said, "Let us also go, that we may die with him" (John 11:16).

860.

In John's Gospel, Jesus describes being born again as "receiving" him. The original word is used to describe a man taking a wife or adopting a child, constituting a committed, lifelong relationship with another.

861.

Mark 16 states that just before Jesus returned to heaven, he told his followers that they would have new powers because of their faith: They would be able to cast out demons, speak in new languages, handle deadly snakes, and drink poison with no harm.

862.

Christians believe that Jesus' death in the New Testament was predicted in the Old Testament. Zechariah refers to his betrayal by a friend, specifying the price of 30 silver shekels. Other passages foretell his silent conduct and acceptance of his fate at trial. And Isaiah 53 gives a vivid description of a divine servant sent to endure suffering, abuse, and death.

863.

Christian tradition states that when Peter was martyred, he asked to be crucified upside down, since he was not worthy to be crucified in the same manner as his Lord was. This may not have been an unusual mode of crucifixion. Some evidence suggests that condemned criminals may have had their heels nailed together and their legs hung over the top of the cross.

864.

The death of Jesus' mother, Mary, is not mentioned in scripture.

865.

About ten years after the Resurrection, the Roman emperor Claudius issued a law making it a capital crime to disturb a burial place. A copy of the law, carved in marble, was found in Nazareth. It is thought the law was in response to the official Jewish explanation of the Resurrection.

866.

The Roman Empire was fairly peaceful for the first 30 or so years after Jesus died. His followers were barely noticed as they established churches from Damascus to Rome by about A.D. 63, when widespread persecution began under Nero. There was some persecution by Jewish leaders, however, including one who would eventually become the Apostle Paul.

867.

In Luke 21:24, Jesus claims of the Jews that "they shall fall by the edge of the sword, and shall be led away captive into all nations: and Jerusalem shall be trodden down of the Gentiles, until the times of the Gentiles be fulfilled." A few decades after Jesus' death, the Romans began the persecution of the Jews that would last for two millennia.

868.

The fish was an early symbol of Christianity, since the Greek word for fish, *icthus*, is an acronym for the Greek phrase *Iesous Christos Theou Huios Soter*, which means "Jesus Christ, of God the Son, Savior." It was written as graffiti, and was used as a secret password when Christians were being persecuted by the Romans.

869.

Abercius, a second-century bishop, wrote that churches often ate bread and fish at communion, a reference to Jesus feeding the 5,000. Newly-baptized Christians were also referred to as "little fish."

870.

A common presumption is that Christianity built its early base through appeal to the vast Roman lower classes. In reality, however, this was not true. Scriptural descriptions of the early Christian church's membership, though sketchy, refer to a variety of social classes. While not many early Christians were wealthy, that was true of overall Roman demographics.

871.

Matthew's gospel did not recount Jesus being taken up to heaven after his post-Resurrection appearances. Matthew's gospel ends with Jesus commissioning his disciples to go out to teach and baptize (Matthew 28:16–20).

872.

The idea of the Trinity is based upon passages such as Matthew 28:19, which says, "Go ye therefore, and teach all nations, baptizing them in the name of the Father, and of the Son, and of the Holy Ghost."

873.

The book of John ends with a verse which tells us that there is so much more to the story of Jesus than we know: "And there are also many other things which Jesus did, the which, if they should be written every one, I suppose that even the world itself could not contain the books that would be written" (John 21:25).

874.

The Acts of the Apostles, written by the same Luke as the Gospel, provides a bridge between the Gospels and Paul's letters to the growing group of believers after Jesus' death. After describing the beginning of the church in Jerusalem, Luke recounts Paul's three missionary journeys into what are now Turkey, Greece, and Italy.

875.

The book of Acts tells the story of the early Christian church. Luke showed the movement of the newly proclaimed message of Jesus Christ from its roots in Judaism and the city of Jerusalem to its transformation into a worldwide, inclusive faith that reached all the way to Rome.

876.

Luke wrote his Gospel and the book of Acts to a Roman official named Theophilus. Much of Acts was written from Luke's own experiences as he traveled with Paul, and the Gospel he wrote while living near Jerusalem benefited from many firsthand accounts, including those of Jesus' mother Mary and half-brother James.

877.

Luke was a companion of the Apostle Paul and may have studied medicine in Tarsus at the same time Paul studied philosophy and law. There are similarities in their language and themes, and both authors were influenced by Greek styles of writing.

878.

Many important decisions in biblical times were made by drawing lots. The sacrificial goat on the Day of Atonement was chosen by lot, and the promised land was apportioned by lot. Achan was revealed by lot as the man responsible for Israel's defeat at Ai, and Saul was chosen Israel's first king by lot. In the New Testament, soldiers cast lots for Jesus' garments, and the disciple who replaced Judas Iscariot was selected by lot.

879.

Matthias replaced Judas as one of the twelve apostles. After Judas's betrayal and death, the other apostles narrowed the choice to Matthias and Joseph (called Barsabas). They prayed and cast lots, and Matthias was chosen (Acts 1:23–26).

880.

The festival of Pentecost takes its name from a Greek word that means "fifty." It was celebrated fifty days after the consecration of the barley harvest on the second day of Passover. It was also called the Feast of Weeks. It took on special significance for the early church when 120 disciples were filled with the Holy Spirit on Pentecost following Christ's resurrection.

881.

On the day of Pentecost, Jesus' followers were together in a house when a mighty wind rushed upon them, flames of fire rested on each of them, and they each began to "speak in tongues" (in languages they did not know). Jews from many different countries were in Jerusalem at the time, and each heard Jesus' followers speaking in their own language. This was a sign of the Holy Spirit's presence.

882.

Baptism with water was an integral part of the early Christians' lives. Peter preached, "Repent, and be baptized every one of you in the name of Jesus Christ for the remission of sins" (Acts 2:38).

883.

In Acts 6:13–14, Stephen was brought before a council for speaking "blasphemous words against this holy place, and the law" and claiming that Jesus would "destroy this place," and "change the customs which Moses delivered." He proceeded to deliver a long indictment of these leaders, accusing them of complicity in Jesus' death.

884.

After he was dragged out of the city and stoned to death, Stephen became the first Christian martyr (Acts 6:8–8:2).

885.

A relatively common ancient death penalty was stoning. Acts 7 mentions that Stephen was stoned for preaching the Gospel to an angry mob. And a passage in Hebrews 11 describes another terrible punishment: being cut in two.

886.

Saul consented to and witnessed Stephen's death. Saul would later become the apostle Paul and one of the greatest missionaries (Acts 8:1).

887.

The English word "simony" refers to the practice of buying or selling ecclesiastical pardons or offices. It comes from Simon the Magician, who tried to buy spiritual power from the apostles after he saw them laying hands on people and the people receiving the Holy Spirit (Acts 8).

888.

In Acts 8:26–40, the Spirit told Philip to leave his ministry in Samaria and "go toward the south." When he did, he encountered an Ethiopian official sitting in his chariot puzzling over scriptures. Philip told him about Jesus and baptized him. Then, "when they were come up out of the water, the Spirit of the Lord caught away Philip." The evangelist "was found" at another town and continued his ministry.

889.

When Saul, later Paul, heard Jesus speak to him outside Damascus, he was struck blind. He remained without sight for three days, and only regained his sight when the disciple Ananias put his hands upon him (Acts 9:8).

890.

Saul, an opponent of the church, was on his way to arrest Christians in Damascus, but he was converted. Now his former colleagues were plotting to kill him. Normal escape routes were too dangerous, so Saul's new friends "took him by night, and let him down by the wall in a basket" (Acts 9:25). After that, Saul (later known as Paul) rushed off to Jerusalem and decades of effective ministry.

891.

Tabitha, a disciple of Jesus, died in the city of Joppa when Peter was in a neighboring town. Tabitha was loved by the community, as she "was full of good works and almsdeeds" (Acts 9:36). The widows especially missed her, and they showed Peter many of the garments she had made for them.

892.

The book of Acts describes how Peter prayed to restore the disciple Dorcas, also known as Tabitha, to life (Acts 9:36–42).

893.

While at Simon the Tanner's house, Peter had a vision in which he was told to eat "unclean" foods, leading to his understanding that the gospel message was to be spread to the Gentiles (Acts 10).

894.

Antioch was the first city in which Jesus' followers were referred to as Christians (Acts 11:26).

895.

Tradition says that most of the apostles died as martyrs. The first to die was James, beheaded by Herod Agrippa in A.D. 44 in Jerusalem. This is the only account of a disciple's death actually recorded in Scripture (Acts 12:1–2). Others are believed to have preached as far away as Ethiopia and India before eventually being killed.

896.

The sorcerer and false prophet that Saul and Barnabas found in Cyprus is called Barjesus in Acts 13:6, but Elymas in Acts 13:8.

897.

It is not known exactly when, where, or why Saul's name was changed to Paul. The transition occurs in Acts 13:9, after which time Paul is the name used to refer to him. It is still unclear if God or Paul himself was responsible for the name change.

898.

When Paul and Barnabas went to Lystra (in Asia Minor, present-day Turkey), they healed a lame man. The crowds were so impressed that they called Barnabas Zeus (the lord of all the Greek gods) and Paul they called Hermes (Zeus' son and spokesman for all the gods), since he was the main speaker of the two (Acts 14:12). The people tried to offer sacrifices to them, but the two restrained them from doing so.

899.

Paul was stoned and left for dead at Lystra (Acts 14:19). Stoning was a form of ritual execution for certain proscribed crimes. These crimes included sacrificing a child to the god Molech, practicing witchcraft, blaspheming God's holy name, and leading people astray to worship other gods. Stoning was also a product of mob violence.

900.

Church elders in Jerusalem chose Silas and Judas Barsabas to go to Antioch, as both were "chief men among the brethren" (Acts 15:22).

901.

Macedonia was the first place in Europe that the Gospel was preached. It was a region of northern Greece and was for many years an independent kingdom. Its most glorious period came under Alexander the Great and his father Philip in the fourth century B.C. Paul was moved to preach there by a vision (Acts 16:9).

902.

Acts 16:9 specifically explains what incites Paul to first journey to Greece: "And a vision appeared to Paul in the night; There stood a man of Macedonia, and prayed him, saying, Come over into Macedonia, and help us."

903.

Lydia was a merchant from Thyatira, and she sold purple cloth. She is described as a worshipper of God, identifying her as a Gentile who was attracted to Judaism. When she met Paul, she was living in Philippi and was attending a prayer meeting with other women by the river. After listening to what Paul had to say, she became the first European convert to Christianity.

904.

The New Testament mentions two earthquakes. One was on the day of Jesus' crucifixion just after he died (Matthew 27:51–53), and the other occurred when Paul and Silas were imprisoned at Philippi (Acts 16:26).

905.

While Paul and Silas were imprisoned in Philippi, a great earthquake shook the foundation of the prison. Even though the doors were opened, Paul and Silas refused to flee, which prompted the jail keeper to ask them what he needed to do to be saved (Acts 16:25–30).

906.

Acts 17:18 mentions Stoic philosophers who argued with Paul at Athens, where they challenged his view of the resurrection of the dead. Paul even quoted a Stoic poet, Aratus, in his argument (Acts 17:28). Stoic philosophy concentrated upon logic, physics, and ethics.

907.

At first the Romans could not distinguish between the Jews and the Christians. The Emperor Claudius, for example, expelled the Jews from Rome in A.D. 49 because of a disturbance over someone named "Chrestus," a misspelling of Christus (Christ). This exile brought Priscilla and Aquila to Corinth, where they met the Apostle Paul (Acts 18:1–4).

908.

Priscilla and Aquila were Jews from Corinth who were coworkers with Paul. They instructed Apollos, a gifted teacher, in the ways of Jesus, and they provided hospitality for Paul in their home (Acts 18). Priscilla is usually mentioned first, suggesting to some scholars that she played the leading role in the couple's ministry.

909.

In Acts 18, Paul sailed from Corinth to Ephesus. The ruins of Ephesus are located on Turkey's western coast.

910.

Acts 18:2 states that one of Paul's traveling companions, Aquila, was "born in Pontus." Pontus is located on the Black Sea's southern shore. On a contemporary map, the region would fall mostly within Turkey's northern border.

911.

The Apostle Paul worked as a tentmaker and generally paid his own way, not depending on collections from the congregations he established. Tentmaking was also a great way to meet travelers. If they accepted the gospel, they would spread it.

912.

Acts 19 mentions a riot instigated by the Apostle Paul's presence at Ephesus, which spilled over into the great Roman theater there. This theater is typical of the countless fine Roman and Greek theaters built throughout Mediterranean lands. These theaters held large crowds but still had perfect sight lines for the audience and were models of good acoustics.

913.

The book of Acts describes how people would bring handkerchiefs or items of clothing that had touched Paul to the sick, who would then be healed (Acts 19:11–12).

914.

In Acts 19:11–20, seven young men, who attempted to wield power to exorcise demons, used the names of Jesus and Paul in their incantations over a demonized man. The demon overpowered all of them, telling them that while it knew about Jesus and Paul, it knew nothing of them. Acts reports that the seven exorcists ran from the house naked and bleeding.

915.

The Bible records two occasions on which books were burned. King Jehoiakim of Judah burned the book of Jeremiah (Jeremiah 36:23). A number of magicians at Ephesus, who were converted as a result of Paul's preaching, brought their books of magic together and burned them publicly (Acts 19:19).

916.

The silversmith felt Paul's arrival in Ephesus might cut into his profits. Demetrius' silver shrines to the goddess Diana "brought no small gain." Paul had preached that gods made with hands are no gods (Acts 19:24–26).

917.

In Acts 20:9–12, Paul was preaching when a young man named Eutychus fell three stories from a window and died. Fortunately, Paul was able to immediately raise him back to life.

918.

Gentiles were not allowed to pass beyond the outer courtyard of the temple. This restriction, along with a misunderstanding, sparked a riot in which Paul was arrested. He had been seen around town with a gentile friend, and when Paul was spotted later in the temple, his enemies assumed the gentile was with him. People "ran together" and dragged Paul out of the temple. His arrest by Roman soldiers probably saved his life (Acts 21:27–36).

919.

The Apostle Paul was born in Tarsus. Tarsus was a city of Cilicia (Acts 21:39).

920.

Acts and Galatians both mention a place named Cilicia. Cilicia was located in southern Turkey, along the coast of the Mediterranean Sea.

921.

While sailing to Italy, Paul's ship was driven off course and shipwrecked on Melita. This island is now known as Malta (Acts 28:1).

922.

After a shipwreck, Paul was bitten by a snake, yet suffered no harm (Acts 28:3–6).

923.

Acts 28:12–13 state that Paul went from Syracuse to Rhegium to Puteoli. Syracuse is on the island of Sicily. Rhegium and Puteoli are on Italy's mainland.

924.

The Apostle Paul spent much time in prison for his faith, and there he wrote several letters to churches. In these letters, he encouraged three different churches to know clearly what they believed and to put these beliefs into practice.

925.

The book of Romans is a letter written to Christians in Rome to explain Paul's understanding of what the Christian faith was about. This book is the most systematic and theological of his letters. The first half emphasizes the theme of righteousness and how to attain it, and the last chapters are practical exhortations about living.

926.

Our word "barbarian" comes from the Greek *barbaros*, which referred to a foreigner, someone speaking an unintelligible language. It is found in Romans 1:14, referring to non-Greeks. The word arose to imitate the way a foreign tongue sounded to Greek ears, a stammering, unknown sound. Originally, it had no insulting connotation at all.

927.

In the Old Testament, the Israelites would sacrifice an animal so humans wouldn't have to pay for their sins in blood. A high priest would sprinkle sacrificial goat's blood on the Ark of the Covenant and then lay hands on the goat to transfer Israel's sin into the "scapegoat." In Romans 3, Paul uses this analogy to explain Jesus' death as atonement "in his blood" for all human sin.

928.

Adoption was common in Roman culture. Under Roman law, the adoptee left his old status and entered into a new relationship with his new father. He had the rights and responsibilities of any natural-born children. Paul used this imagery to portray what happens to new believers: They are adopted into God's family as his own children (Romans 8).

929.

Romans 8:28 says, "And we know that all things work together for good to them that love God, to them who are the called according to his purpose." Too many believers edit this verse to "all things work together for good." When we consider the verse within its chapter, we find that it's a powerful truth rooted in God's eternal purposes. The Lord is working on a greater plan—and it's often different from our plans.

930.

Paul sent Phebe to Rome and asked that she be received "in the Lord, as becometh saints" and that she be assisted "in whatsoever business she hath need of" (Romans 16:1–2).

931.

Women do not always feature prominently in the Bible, but Paul had many female associates. Phebe was a deacon and benefactor, Prisca hosted a church in her house, and Junia spent time with Paul in prison. There was Tryphena and Tryphosa, "who labour in the Lord," and a hard-working woman named Mary (Romans 16:1–12). Paul acknowledges that Euodias and Synthche struggled beside him (Philippians 4:2–3). And in Philippi, Paul made his headquarters in the home of Lydia, a woman he had baptized.

932.

The church at Corinth, Greece, had many problems. Paul's letters to them—there were at least four, but only two are preserved—address their issues one by one. These issues included factions in the church, incest, marriage, food offered to idols, spiritual gifts (such as speaking in unintelligible tongues), opposition to Paul, and the concept of resurrection.

933.

The ancient city of Corinth was located on the narrow isthmus that connects the Peloponnese peninsula to the mainland.

934.

The "church" in Corinth consisted of small groups that met in the homes of the wealthier members. Paul sent letters to these house churches because a number of the converts had difficulty leaving behind their pre-Christian ways. "First" Corinthians was not actually the first letter Paul sent. Paul makes mention of a previous letter (1 Corinthians 5:9) that occasioned some misunderstanding that he clarifies in this letter.

935.

In 1 Corinthians 9:24–27, Paul speaks of physical training and running races. The people of the Bible were very much like us, and they enjoyed the competition and fellowship of participating in contests that challenged them physically and mentally.

936.

Christian tradition followed Greek custom: Men's heads were not to be covered during worship (1 Corinthians 11:4). Indeed, this was a sign of dishonor to God. Women, however, were to have their heads covered as a sign of honor (11:5–6). Scholars disagree whether Paul meant that a woman's head covering was to be a veil or shawl, or merely long hair.

937.

Several times Jesus prophesied about a baptism that would come from the Holy Spirit. John the Baptist stated that his baptism was with water, but Jesus' was different: "He shall baptize you with the Holy Ghost, and with fire" (Matthew 3:11). Paul spoke of being "baptized into one body" by one Spirit (1 Corinthians 12:13). This means that Christians would be filled and covered with the Spirit as they were covered by water in baptism.

938.

Paul's great reflections on charity are found in 1 Corinthians 13. At the end of his discussion, he stresses that "faith, hope, charity" are the greatest of all gifts, but he concludes that "the greatest of these is charity."

939.

The Apostle Paul said that we perceive heavenly things imperfectly, as "through a glass, darkly; but then face to face" (1 Corinthians 13:12).

940.

Belial was not originally a name, but it developed into a name for Satan in Jewish literature in the period between the Testaments. The Apostle Paul used the word in this way when he asked "And what concord hath Christ with Belial?" (2 Corinthians 6:15).

941.

The Apostle Paul mentioned a "thorn in the flesh" that was given to him to keep him from pride (2 Corinthians 12:7). He asked God three times about it, but it was never removed. Scholars have speculated almost endlessly about what it was. Suggestions include earaches, headaches, eye afflictions, epilepsy, hysteria, malaria, speech impediment, or human enemies. Unfortunately, we do not know what his problem was.

942.

The apostle Paul asked God three times to remove his "thorn in the flesh." Finally, God responded, "My grace is sufficient for thee: for my strength is made perfect in weakness" (2 Corinthians 12:9).

943.

Paul addresses "the churches of Galatia" in Galatians 1:2. Galatia was located in the central and northern interior highlands of modern-day Turkey.

944.

An allegory is a story that carries a hidden meaning, or, more commonly, several hidden meanings. A well-known example is from the Apostle Paul, when he speaks of Abraham's two wives, Sarah and Hagar. He says, "Which things are an allegory: for these are the two covenants; the one from the mount Sinai, which gendereth to bondage, which is Agar" (Galatians 4:24). He also compares Hagar with the earthly Jerusalem and Sarah with the heavenly city.

945.

The Holy Spirit appears throughout the Bible. Paul describes two important activities of the Holy Spirit—the gifts of the Spirit and the fruits of the Spirit. Every believer has at least one special ability granted by the Spirit for the glory of God (1 Corinthians 12:7–11). And when a believer is guided by God's Spirit, the resulting "fruit" is love, joy, peace, patience, kindness, generosity, faithfulness, gentleness, and self-control (Galatians 5:22–23).

946.

Paul had a special love for the church in Ephesus, where he spent over two years. We see his affection in the poetic prayer included in Ephesians 3:14–21. He wanted them to be "rooted and grounded in love," to know "the breadth, and length, and depth, and height" of Christ's love, which "passeth knowledge."

947.

Philippians is written to "the servants of Jesus Christ, to all the saints in Christ Jesus which are at Philippi," as noted in the epistle's first verse. The city's ruins are located in the northeastern region of Macedonia.

948.

The Apostle Paul occasionally used the words of early Christian hymns in writing his letters. The most famous example is in Philippians 2:5–11, where a soaring passage about Christ's humility, humiliation, and ultimate exaltation is found.

949.

There have always been crude, loudmouthed, insulting people, even in biblical times. James 4:11 pleads, "Speak not evil one of another, brethren." And Paul urged the Colossians to "put off all these; anger, wrath, malice, blasphemy, filthy communication out of your mouth" (Colossians 3:8).

950.

Paul instructed his readers to include music in their worship. He says, "Let the word of Christ dwell in you richly in all wisdom; teaching and admonishing one another in psalms and hymns and spiritual songs, singing with grace in your hearts to the Lord" (Colossians 3:16). These included the words of Scripture (psalms), as well as songs of praise (hymns) and other types of songs (spiritual songs).

951.

The Thessalonians that Paul's epistle addresses were inhabitants of Thessalonica, which falls in Greece's northeastern region of Macedonia.

952.

Paul gave the church at Thessalonica, Greece, encouragement and instruction in 1 and 2 Thessalonians. This included much teaching about the return of Christ to earth at the end of time.

953.

In 1 Thessalonians, Paul speaks of Jesus' return. Scholars suspect that some of the Thessalonian Christians took Paul's words about the "rapture" too far, quitting their jobs or taking other drastic measures to await the Lord's return. So it makes sense that Paul's second letter to this church mentions signs that will precede Jesus' coming (2 Thessalonians 2:1–12).

954.

1 and 2 Timothy were addressed to two people who were ministers (pastors) of churches. The letters gave specific instructions about the orderly functioning of churches and for resisting false teachings.

955.

Paul had many people who helped and encouraged him in his ministry. One was Onesiphorus, who often "refreshed" Paul. When Paul was imprisoned in Rome, Onesiphorus went to Rome and eagerly looked for him until he found him, where he encouraged Paul greatly. Paul contrasted Onesiphorus' example with that of Phygellus and Hermogenes, who abandoned him and the gospel he preached (2 Timothy 1:15–18 and 2:17–18).

956.

For Romans, a punishment meant a beating, execution, or even exile, while prison was simply a place to wait for a trial. This is why Paul still had his own house in Rome where guests were welcome. Roman citizens were usually only chained when being moved from place to place.

957.

You may have heard that "money is the root of all evil." Not exactly. It's the *love* of money: "For the love of money is the root of all evil" (1 Timothy 6:10).

958.

Timothy was inspired and influenced by the "unfeigned faith" of his grandmother, Lois, and his mother, Eunice (2 Timothy 1:5).

959.

An example where Paul actually invented a new word is *Theopneustos*, which means "God-breathed." This is formed by combining *Theos* ("God") and *pneuma* ("breath"). The word was not used in Paul's day, but he coined the term to describe the nature of Scripture: It was "God-breathed," meaning the very words of God (2 Timothy 3:16). Usually *Theopneustos* is translated as "inspiration of God."

960.

From 2 Timothy 4:10, we learn that Titus, one of Paul's companions, had left him to go to Dalmatia. This was a Roman district in what is today Croatia. It is thought to be the original home of the dalmatian breed of dog.

961.

One of Paul's most intensely personal letters is a friendly, tactful letter to his friend Philemon, who owned a runaway slave, Onesimus. This slave had been captured, and he converted to Christianity under Paul in prison. Paul asked Philemon to welcome the slave as he would welcome Paul.

962.

Paul wanted Onesimus to be on his mission team, so he sent the slave back to his owner, Philemon, with a letter requesting his freedom. The name Onesimus means "profitable," and Paul played with this idea, telling Philemon that even though Philemon once considered him "useless" as a slave, Onesimus had become "useful" in Paul's ministry.

963.

Most New Testament letter writers identify themselves. Only one—Hebrews—departs from this norm. Foregoing greetings, it dives right into its teachings. The only unidentified New Testament author wrote the Bible's premier chapter on faith. Hebrews 11 begins, "Now faith is the substance of things hoped for, the evidence of things not seen."

964.

The author of Hebrews forcefully makes the point that Jesus was the perfect fulfillment of much prophecy in the Old Testament.

965.

Whereas Romans, Galatians, and Hebrews stress the importance of faith alone in one's relationship to God, the book of James presents the case that faith without good works to demonstrate this faith is dead intellectualism.

966.

The Apostle Peter's two letters offer encouragement to those suffering persecution. Peter reminds them of their fellow sufferer and the perfect example, Jesus. These letters also warn against false teachings.

967.

In 1 Peter 3:19, the author speaks of Jesus preaching "unto the spirits in prison" between his own death and resurrection. This verse came to be interpreted as an indication that Jesus preached the gospel to those who had died before his coming, giving them an opportunity to believe and be released from hell.

968.

According to Peter, "charity" covers a multitude of sins (1 Peter 4:8).

969.

Christ is the true "morning star" in the New Testament. He is called this in 2 Peter 1:19 ("the day star arise in your hearts") and Revelation 22:16 ("I am the root and the offspring of David, and the bright and morning star"). These allusions pick up on such Old Testament passages as Numbers 24:17: "There shall come a Star out of Jacob."

970.

John's letters deal with truth in the face of false teaching, especially early Gnosticism (intellectual knowledge can lead to salvation). In his first letter, he also emphasizes right relationship with God through Jesus Christ, and the importance of love in all areas of our life.

971.

Jude warns against false teachings, much in the way that 2 Peter does. A distinctive aspect of Jude is that it quotes from non-biblical books, such as the Assumption of Moses (in verse 9) and the book of Enoch (in verse 14).

972.

The book of Revelation presents the Apostle John's visions of the end of time. The book is rich with symbols and strange creatures, great armies and cataclysmic battles, a lake of fire, and a bottomless pit. The consistent message of the book is the ultimate and final triumph of Christ over the devil and all forces of evil.

973.

The book of Revelation is the longest example of apocalyptic literature in the Bible. It speaks of great hosts of angels and a great red dragon with seven heads and ten horns and seven crowns on its heads. It describes several beasts, one that looked like a leopard with feet like a bear's and a mouth like a lion's. The dragon and the beasts are symbols of the devil.

974.

Eight verses into the book of Revelation, God says, "I am Alpha and the Omega." *Alpha* and *omega* are the first and last letters of the Greek alphabet. So the Lord was declaring his presence at the beginning and the end of human history. This phrase occurs twice more, uttered by "he that sat upon the throne" (God the Father) and by Jesus (Revelation 21:5–6, 22:13).

975.

The first chapter of Revelation states, "I John… was in the isle that is called Patmos, for the word of God, and for the testimony of Jesus Christ" (Revelation 1:9). Patmos was one of several Aegean islands used by the Romans for exile, especially for soothsayers and prophets. If John talked about his Revelation visions before his exile, it would explain why he was sent to Patmos.

976.

The prophetic author of Revelation calls himself "John to the seven churches which are in Asia," and is assumed by most scholars to be the apostle John. However, some theologians disagree with that assumption, suggesting instead that the author may actually have been a disciple of John.

977.

In Revelation 1:13–16, the author describes one "like unto the Son of man" who held "in his right hand seven stars: and out of his mouth went a sharp twoedged sword: and his countenance was as the sun shineth in his strength." Revelation 1:20 says that the seven stars represent the angels of the seven churches whom the author was called to address.

978.

Only one Bible writer describes Jesus' appearance, and this is only after Jesus returns to heaven. In Revelation, the last book in the Bible, the Apostle John says, "his head and his hairs were white like wool. . . and his eyes as a flame of fire; And his feet like unto fine brass, as if they burned in a furnace; and his voice as the sound of many waters" (1:14–15).

979.

The name Jesus appears 700 times in the Gospels, which tell the story of his life. However, it appears less than 70 times in the epistles. On the other hand, the name Christ appears about 60 times in the Gospels and the book of Acts, while it occurs 240 times in the epistles and the book of Revelation.

980.

The book of Revelation mentions the doctrine of the Nicolaitanes, "which thing I [Jesus] hate" (Revelation 2:15). Nicolaitanes were associated with the teaching of Balaam, who encouraged the Israelites to practice immorality and eat food offered to idols. This was in precise violation of an apostolic decree (Acts 15:20).

981.

Eliakim was made the grand vizier over the household of King Hezekiah (Isaiah 22:15–25). He was given "the key of the house of David" to wear on his shoulder. This symbolized his exclusive authority to grant access to the king. This image is picked up in Revelation 3:7, where Christ now has "the key of David," and he alone now grants access to God.

982.

The book of Revelation isn't all about strange beasts and conflicts. The first few chapters contain messages to specific churches from Jesus. To one church he says: "Behold, I stand at the door, and knock: if any man hear my voice, and open the door, I will come in to him, and will sup with him, and he with me" (Revelation 3:20).

983.

In Revelation 5:13, "every creature which is in heaven, and on the earth, and under the earth, and such as are in the sea," are described as singing "Blessing, and honour, and glory and power, be unto him that sitteth upon the throne, and unto the Lamb."

984.

There are hundreds of names for Jesus in the Bible. In Revelation 5:5, Jesus is called "the Lion of the tribe of Judah, the Root of David."

985.

Revelation 6 mentions four magnificent horses and their riders, representing the evils to come at the end of the world. The first horse was white, representing conquest; the second, red, representing war; the third, black, representing famine. The fourth horse was pale, its rider's name was Death. It represented war, famine, pestilence, and wild beasts all at once.

986.

In Revelation, Apollyon is referred to as the angel of the bottomless pit and the king of an army of locusts that appear as fearsome war horses with human faces, lion's teeth, and scalelike breast plates. There has been some debate among theologians as to whether Apollyon is good or evil.

987.

Dragons are found in both the Old and New Testaments. In the Old Testament, the term is sometimes more accurately translated as serpent, but often it refers to the great monster of mythology. It is a symbol of evil. In Revelation 12, it is a symbol of Satan.

988.

Michael is an archangel who disputed with Satan in Jude 1:9. Michael's role was less a messenger (such as Gabriel) and more an angelic defender who led armies of angels against the forces of evil. In Revelation 12:7, Michael and his angels fought the great, evil dragon and its forces.

989.

The beast's number is 666 (Revelation 13:18). This has led to endless speculation about the beast's identity. Some people have used various methods of assigning numbers to letters. Many early interpreters thought individual Roman emperors were being referred to. Being one digit short of the triple number of perfection—777—it symbolizes evil's perversion and falling short of the true standard of perfection.

990.

In Revelation 16:12, an angel pours out a vial in the Euphrates River, causing it to dry up.

991.

Like any good story, Revelation features several compelling characters. These include a heroic Jesus; his adversary, Satan (who is referred to by many names in Revelation, including "the dragon," "the Beast," and the "False Prophet"); the archangel Michael; the Four Horsemen of the Apocalypse; and the Whore of Babylon, who is not a woman, but rather a reference to Rome.

992.

In the book of Revelation, John paints a picture of a corrupt, bloodthirsty Rome. However, he does not refer to Rome by name, thus avoiding any charge of insurrection by the Roman authorities. Instead, he names Babylon, but readers during his day would comprehend the true identity of "Babylon."

993.

In the rich imagery of Revelation, Jesus is portrayed as the sacrificial Lamb, but at the end of the story, he's very much alive—and he's getting married. The church is described as his bride, and the world ends with a party to end all parties—a reception, if you will. "Blessed are they which are called unto the marriage supper of the Lamb" (Revelation 19:9).

994.

The book of Revelation mentions a lake of fire. John assures us in multiple places that the ultimate destination of sundry devils, beasts, and false prophets—along with anyone whose name is not written in the book of life—is this lake (Revelation 19:20, 20:10, 14, 15, and 21:8).

995.

The book of Revelation describes a future war between God and Satan, in which the devil loses and is imprisoned for a thousand years. He then returns to power, but God again defeats him, and the devil is "cast into the lake of fire and brimstone" where he "shall be tormented day and night for ever and ever" (Revelation 20:10). Even through Revelation's confusing imagery, one thing is clear: God triumphs over evil.

996.

The most commonly mentioned heavenly book is the Book of Life. It refers to the keeping of an account of those who are truly believers and those who are not. In Revelation, those whose names are found written in the Book of Life will escape the everlasting judgment. Most other heavenly books are related to the Book of Life in some way.

997.

John watched New Jerusalem descend from heaven, describing the holy city "coming down from God out of heaven, prepared as a bride adorned for her husband" (Revelation 21:2).

998.

About 30 different types of precious stones are mentioned in the Bible. They include multicolored agates, reddish-purple amethysts, green emeralds, red garnets, clear diamonds, shiny pearls, red rubies, and blue sapphires. Revelation describes the New Jerusalem with precious gems lodged in its gates and walls (Revelation 21:18–21).

999.

In the Apostle John's vision of heavenly Jerusalem (Revelation 21 and 22), he saw a shimmering, bejeweled city descend from heaven. The city was a spectacular fantasy, however, since it was a perfect cube measuring 1,500 miles on each side—the distance from New York to Houston. It was clearly symbolic of the glories that lay ahead.

1000.

Genesis 2:9 describes how God placed a tree called the "tree of life" in the middle of the Garden of Eden as a symbol of eternal life. This same tree is described once again at the end of the Bible. Revelation describes the tree of life growing in the New Jerusalem, bearing 12 kinds of fruit. Its leaves are used for healing (Revelation 22:2).